CW01432830

MY SUICIDE NOTE

MY
SUICIDE
NOTE

searching for purpose

JOHN MILLER

PALMETTO
PUBLISHING

Charleston, SC
www.PalmettoPublishing.com

My Suicide Note
Copyright © 2023 by John Miller

All rights reserved
No portion of this book may be reproduced, stored in a retrieval system, or transmitted
in any form by any means–electronic, mechanical, photocopy, recording, or other–except
for brief quotations in printed reviews, without prior permission of the author.

First Edition

Hardcover: 979-8-8229-1440-7
Paperback: 979-8-8229-1441-4
eBook: 979-8-8229-1442-1

Contents

Foreword

This book is sure to be therapy for the soul. I know it was written as a form of lifesaving therapy for its author. Anyone who was, has, or is suffering from soul-crippling depression should read this book. Depression is a life stealer. It has the power to destroy a life like a fire mercilessly destroys everything in its path. A raging fire consumes everything and leaves nothing behind but piles of ashes. I know this firsthand as fire destroyed my in-laws' home leaving nothing behind. I have also watched helplessly as depression engulfed the life of my friend like a fire burning everything that was precious and leaving only ashes. However, from out of those ashes I am watching a phoenix rise. This is the story of triumph from tragedy. It is both awful and awesome memoir. It is both beautiful and brutal narrative. Above all it is honest.

My name is Mike Conaway and I have been privileged to be in a three-decade-long friendship with the author John Miller. John and I began this lifelong friendship during his internship at a local church in Dade City, Florida, during his college days at Southeastern University of the Assemblies of God. The local church was my home church and John came to volunteer with a mutual friend and staff member at the church. John served for two or more semesters at the church interning. I would later go on to step out in faith and answer God's call on my life to ministry and join John and our mutual friend from the church at Southeastern University.

John is younger than I am. I got a late start in my relationship with God. My path was forged through a life of adversity due to heavy drug and alcohol abuse. I found Jesus, or I should say, Jesus found me and changed my life in dramatic fashion. So, John started ministry school and finished ministry school a few years ahead of me. While he was younger, it did not keep us from becoming friends.

John and I became fast friends. Our friendship was quick to take shape because of our mutual love of professional football. He is a die-hard San Francisco 49ers fan and I am a die-hard fan of the Dallas Cowboys. Anybody who knows football knows the 49ers and the Cowboys share a storied rivalry. Just mention "The Catch" to any true fan and they will know what I am talking about. The rivalry between these two teams was the common ground that helped us to forge what has become a three-decade-long friendship. John and I were pastors in training with a desire to see healthy changes come into the church. Our hope was to help people focus less on religion and more on a relationship with Jesus. I ministered in Florida, North Carolina, and Texas while John ministered in Virginia, Washington, and Oregon. No matter where we were, we were committed to stay in touch to offer wisdom, encouragement, and support.

John and I have remained friends throughout the years as we have traveled and ministered in numerous states, pastoral roles, and churches. We found great value in our relationship, so we chose to invest the time and energy to stay connected. Ministry is a very lonely existence. The life of a minister is extremely stressful in many ways. You give yourself away piece by piece as you love and serve people. Ministers are there during the most stressful times in the lives of those in their community. Compassion fatigue can set in and create excruciating guilt and shame. Divorce, death, and disease are constant as is the desire to please people. Truthfully, the desire to please people and keep "the sheep" happy, or at least at bay, is an ever-present impossible challenge. Ministers live with the reality that your ministry can be totally destroyed by someone other than you on any given Sunday. It takes its toll on the soul.

The reason this book is so critical is because the aforementioned lonely and stressful life left my friend broken in ways that you will have to read to believe. This book has been written as a part of the ongoing healing process for John. It was written from the heart of a man who does not want to see anyone go through what he went through alone. It is an honest, transparent, painful memoir written with a strong desire to bring hope to the hopeless and help to those who feel helpless. I have lived this journey step by step with John praying and hoping that I would not lose my friend. There were times, as you will read, where that loss was closer and more imminent than I could have ever even imagined. I could not be happier to have been asked by John to write this foreword. Trust me when I say this: it is so much better than when I was asked to officiate his funeral services. The reason is simple: my friend is still alive! He may not be completely out of the woods yet, but he is still here with us.

There were so many times where this book was the only thread keeping John hanging on. I remember when John told me that he gave his therapist in Hawaii my phone number in the event that something were to happen to him. He asked me to handle all of his final affairs. I cannot tell you the sheer fear that came over my face when my phone rang, and it was the number of his therapist that I had saved in my phone. I looked at the screen on my phone and said, "Oh no, John. Tell me you didn't!" I answered and luckily it was his therapist, but she was not calling to tell me John was gone, she was calling to get vital information to help in John's recovery and therapy. His therapy through this book is what kept him from hanging it up and throwing in the towel. He just kept saying, "Mike, I've got to get this book out of me. I know I am supposed to write this book. I know it is going to help people." There was even a time where I was absolutely terrified because he said, "Mike, you may have to finish the last few chapters. I don't know if I'm gonna make it." I am beyond grateful to God that John's statement did not come true and he was able to stay in the fight and finish this powerful life-giving, potentially lifesaving book. I would highly recommend grabbing a copy of this book to any-one experiencing depression at any level or if you know some-one valiantly battling depression.

I have been right here side by side with John through this horrific fight. He has struggled, clawed, and scratched his way through a literal hell to bring this book into existence. He has lived every heart-wrenching, teeth-clenching second while dan-gling on a high wire over the abyss. The single glimmer of hope that has fueled his ever-flickering life light has been to put his story out into the world in hopes that it could help even one. His hope has been to see his story give someone, anyone, fight-ing for their life a spark in the darkness.

I am proud of John for the selfless way he put his life out there in full. This memoir includes the good, the bad, and the ugly. It is a hard-hitting, truth-telling narrative that reveals just how crafty and devious the adversary known as depression weaves its way into the fabric of our lives.

My favorite part of this story is that it is not OVER! My hope is that my now three-decade-long friendship will extend for decades more, the Good Lord willing, of course.

John, my friend, you are a warrior. Thank you for telling your story. Thank you for not giving up! I thank you for your trust and your friendship.

Still Fighting,
Mike Conaway
Pastor and Friend

Introduction

It was a sunny afternoon in Los Angeles, and I was walking in Santa Monica, not far from the beach, when a young woman in a green T-shirt motioned to me to get my attention. It was my first time on the Third Street Promenade, and I was a little overwhelmed with the amount of activity happening all around me. There were street performers and musicians performing for wealthy Hollywood executives and panhandlers alike, and out of all of this chaos, the young woman came up to me.

"Excuse me, sir," she said. "Can I ask you a question?"

She looked to be about twenty, and she gripped a binder close to her chest. There was a rehearsed smile spread across her face, and I knew she was going to ask me to donate money to a cause before she opened her mouth. I looked around and noticed a few other twentysomethings in the same T-shirt, also stopping people on the street, holding identical binders.

I met her eyes and said, "Tell you what. You can ask me *one* question."

I don't know why I said it, exactly. I think I was just trying to gauge her salesman ability. Could she deliver her entire pitch while only asking one single question?

Turns out, she could.

She was representing a charity for children with cancer, and she gave me a wealth of information about the organization in a few short, concise sentences. She ended her monologue with "So, what do you think?"

I paused, waiting for her to say more, but she didn't. "That's the question?" I said.

"Yep."

"But you didn't ask how much I'd be willing to give."

"Nope," she said. "You said one question, right?"

"Huh."

I took out my wallet and handed her a twenty-dollar bill. I then said, "Do you mind if I tell you something?"

"Sure," she said, nodding.

"As of yesterday," I said, "I'm homeless."

Her face shifted. The rehearsed smile disappeared. She looked at me with concern. "I'm so sorry."

I nodded my thanks.

She looked at the twenty in her hand. "Well," she said, "hopefully this will come back around to you. Karma."

I smiled, thanked her for listening, and moved on.

I walked along the promenade for a while, watching the street performers, taking stock of all the events of my life that had led me to this point. I've lived in many places, from the quiet small towns of Pennsylvania to the beautiful shores of Hawaii, before ending up living out of a hotel room in the tiny town of Quincy, Illinois. What brought me there was a series of events that included starting my own church and attempting to take my own life.

But it all started with my family.

CHAPTER 1

Just One More Home

My father, James, had been a Master Gunnery Sergeant in the
Marine Corps, and he spent every minute of his spare time
working as a pastor. Every weekend and often on some week-
nights, he would take us to church. On many Sundays, we attended church twice, once in the morning and once at night. At
times, we would sleep on the pews between services.

When he retired from the Marine Corps, my uncle
Malcolm, himself a lead pastor at a church in Virginia, arranged
for my dad to work with him as a staff pastor, and so we moved
to a town called Winchester. We had always moved around
when I was growing up since the military took my dad all over
the country (and even to a two-year stint in Japan, though as I
was too young I don't remember it). I'd moved six times by the
age of twelve, and had long stopped feeling like any particular
place was "home."

When we got to Virginia, we became very involved with the
church my uncle ran, which was a part of a grouping of churches called the Assemblies of God.

The Assemblies of God began as a small church of around
three hundred people, founded in Arkansas in 1914. It's now

the largest Pentecostal denomination in the world, with millions of members in the US and abroad, and once we were officially members, it dominated everything about my life. Our schedules revolved around when the church doors were open. When I wasn't in school, I was learning scriptures at home. Attending church services and Sunday School were predetermined events, and there was no getting out of them, ever.

Whether I liked it or not, the Assemblies of God was the institution that would come to shape so much of my life for the next twenty-odd years.

We stayed in Winchester for just a year, and so, when I was twelve, we moved again, this time to Jeannette, Pennsylvania. I had just turned twelve, and now in my adolescence I was really starting to resent the fact that we never stayed in a place long enough for me to make any real friends. I was often lonely, and my family offered no comfort in that area.

I know the conventional image of a churchgoing family includes a lot of group outings, cheery Christmas mornings, and warm, lively conversations over family dinner. But the truth was that just wasn't what my family was like. At all.

My father always seemed far more interested in his work than spending time with any of his children, but like many boys with distant fathers, that only made me more intent on earning his approval. He was never a violent man—he never hit us. But in a way I would have preferred that, because at least it would have meant he took an interest in what we were doing or saying. When you're a child, especially when you're the youngest child of several, it's so important to feel like your voice is heard by your parents. But that was just not in the cards for me.

As for my mother, she can best be summed up by what she most often said to my brothers and me growing up whenever we questioned one of our father's demands or decisions. "Your father's always right," she would tell us. "Even when he's wrong, he's right." My mom would also say, "Everything has its place and every place has its thing." I use that to this day. She was a peacemaker who helped everyone feel good about themselves.

If we were looking for someone to cover for us, we were looking in the wrong place.

My oldest brother, Pete, graduated soon after the move and went straight into the army, and Greg, the second oldest in our family, was a brainy, aloof bookish type who skipped a year of school when we got to Jeannette. Maybe it was because they took a cue from my father, but both of my brothers were cold and distant, and I was never close with either of them growing up.

In Virginia, I had heard from other kids at school and church about how they and their brothers would go fishing with their fathers on the weekends. Some of them even had the nerve to say it was boring and they wished their dads didn't drag them away. They had no idea how good they had it. To have a parent who wanted to spend time with you, or even considered you *worthy* of their time, sounded like winning the lottery to me. With my father, I often felt isolated and alone. Sometimes he sent me along with friends and their dads to join them for fishing excursions, but it only made me more aware of how much I missed him and wished he was with me.

My one activity that I loved growing up was basketball, as it was one of the few times I felt like I could be myself, an individual, accomplishing things that had nothing to do with church. Beyond that, the physical activity, the intensity of the games, was thrilling, and I was actually good at it. Basketball was my thing. It was part of what defined me. I took pride in it.

In all my time playing, my father never really engaged with me about my game.

All that was ever really discussed in our house was God and the church. Like I said, he wasn't a violent man and rarely raised his voice, but he was strict. My father would say he is fair, firm, and friendly. He forced us to obey the rules of the church without question, and the Assemblies of God was not a fun, modern, happy place. It was extremely conservative and austere, and I would often think, as a child, about how eager I was to grow up.

Things improved a bit when we moved to Jeannette, because for the first time in my life, I was able to make some real friends. Unfortunately, the origin of these friendships was intimidation and violence, but you take what you can get.

The middle school in Jeannette was a way rougher place than the school I'd gone to in Virginia, and it took a lot of adjusting to get used to. Kids were always getting into fights and ganging up on each other. I tried to explain the problems of my school to my mom and dad, but it felt like my conversation was ignored. *I* was ignored. So I had no choice but to keep going to school.

I was in seventh grade at the time. In my math class, a guy named Darnell decided for some reason that I would be his enemy and his punching bag. He approached me and told me that he was going to kick my butt after school, and there was nothing I could do about it.

After school that day, I dutifully showed up to the back of the building, where about thirty kids had gathered to watch my inevitable pummeling, wringing their hands in excitement for the impending carnage and chanting "Fight, fight, fight!" Unfortunately, I never gave them the show they or Darnell expected, because I ended up completely beating the crap out of Darnell.

But because Darnell was a tough kid and used to fighting, this didn't further his animosity towards me. Instead, it actually resulted in me winning his respect. He and I became friends, and I soon befriended the other kids in his group, like Rich and Curtis (whom we called Zeus, because of his massive size).

It started with a fight, but then boom—just like that, for the first time ever, I had a group of friends. We probably looked funny, all us running around, a bunch of black kids and one white kid stuck together like glue, but it was some of the best times of my young life.

We would hang out together all the time, spending time at each other's houses and causing trouble throughout the neighborhood. It was through my relationship with them that I realized something about my parents. It turned out that in addition to feeling alone, my parents seemed cautious with my friends.

One time, Rich was over at my place and asked me if we had an iron, so I got him the iron we had in our closet. I also brought the ironing board, figuring he needed to press his shirt or something, but no—this was the late 80s, and so Rich needed to iron his hair into the perfect Kid 'n Play flattop.

I thought that was hilarious and really cool, but my mom had a different opinion. When she learned about this practice being done with her iron, she was not sure what to do.

I wasn't sure how to respond. "Well, my friends probably think we are weird," I eventually replied to her, ending the subject and letting her know exactly where I stood.

I ignored my parents' growing distaste of my friends and just enjoyed my time with them. We played basketball all the time together, and went to the Friday night football games at Jeannette High School. The football games were awesome, and really wild. The Jeannette High School football team was one of the top state football teams at the time, so there was always a huge and enthusiastic crowd. It was the place to be.

My buddies and I would go and talk to the girls there, and we often wound up getting in fights with other boys. Often we went to postgame parties thrown at random kids' houses. It was a wild and raucous time, and the last thing my parents were comfortable with, but that didn't bother me in the slightest. I had friends. I was happy.

One time, a kid in school was talking trash about me and sending vague threats. But I never had to deal with him. Why? Because before news of this even reached my ears, Rich heard about it and beat the crap out of the kid, and the boy never mentioned my name again.

When you messed with one of us, you messed with all of us.

My friends even made the ultimate sacrifice (in my opinion) and came to church services with me, so my parents would see them as good, upstanding young men. They did it just so we could hang out, and if sitting through boring church services that you are questioning isn't the definition of a true bond, I don't know what is.

But despite their newly acquired church habit, anyone could see we weren't choirboys. Like I said, we got in a lot of fights. We smoked pot that another friend got from his dad, who was a dealer and would always have pot around, giving it to us in little ounce bags. We got into all sorts of mischief, and yet it was the healthiest time of my life, emotionally. Now I had people who listened to me when I spoke, and whom I would listen to in return.

One of the things I've learned in my life is that listening to others is something that can never be overvalued. It sounds incredibly simple, but growing up in a family where it felt like no one would listen to a word I said was so damaging. It made me feel like I didn't matter. And the person who probably listened to me the least was my father—at least it felt that way to me.

All the trouble I got into with my friends, all the fights and parties and drugs, I realized I was acting out because I was trying get my dad's attention *somehow*. Even if it was negative, even if it meant he was angry with me, at least I would know he was aware I existed. He was so cold and so distant when I was growing up that, even though I wasn't aware of it at the time, getting him to notice me was my major objective in life. And if he wouldn't pay me any mind when I was a good kid, maybe he would if I was bad.

Like I said, we moved around all the time when I was growing up, so I changed schools the way malls change holiday decorations. But those transfers were always due to us moving.

Until I got kicked out of school for the first time.

It turns out when you get into a lot of fights and make a habit of talking back to teachers, it gets you on the radar of school administrators. Who knew, right? I was in trouble all the time, but the last straw came when some school officials were filming parts of classes for a parent-teacher night presentation or something.

I was in eighth grade by that time, and had established a bad reputation with the school. When one of the staff came in and took a quick pan of our class with their camera, I thought it would be hilarious to flip him off, so I did, raising my middle finger and smirking when the camera got to me.

After some time getting into fights and various other troubles, that did it. The school called in my parents and informed the three of us I was no longer welcome to attend Jeannette Junior High School.

I wish I could say my behavior got better when I went to the strict private school my parents enrolled me in, but that just wasn't the case. By this time I'd grown accustomed to being a bad kid, and the chip on my shoulder was the size of a house. I was rude and disrespectful to teachers, I was disruptive in class, and I was hostile to the other students. I was almost kicked out of that school before the year was even up, but they allowed me to stay and finish out the year.

But I wouldn't be returning, they were sure to tell my parents.

You would think this would cause some kind of intervention on my parents' part, where they tried to get to the root of the problem as to why I was such a bad kid. But no. They just transferred me to another private school, hoped for the best, and went about their lives.

It turned out being a bad kid didn't earn me my father's attention, either, as I would learn year after year. Soon I was in high school, and nothing I'd done worked in getting my father's attention.

He did occasionally weigh in on certain issues, however. My last year in Jeannette, when I was sixteen, I was getting ready to go out with Rich, Zeus, and some other guys for Halloween when my dad told me I wasn't allowed out. It was a Wednesday, and in my house Wednesday night meant I had to go to church (which was in addition to—not in place of—Sunday services).

I couldn't believe it. Years of ignoring me only to stand in my way now. Though his attention was what I craved, the timing made me furious. This was Halloween! A night when sixteen-year-old kids are supposed to misbehave a little. A rage built inside me, sudden and unexpected, and I did something that to this day still surprises me.

My dad was standing in the doorway, blocking my exit, so I shoved him.

Years of fighting and basketball had made me strong and tough, and my dad was no match for me. He stepped back a bit, stunned that I'd laid hands on him, and I just walked right on past, out of the house and over to Rich's. I could barely believe what had happened, but the more I thought about it, the more angry I became. Who was he to tell me what to do?

When I got to Rich's, we all smoked pot and drank beers, and I reveled in feeling so rebellious. The Assemblies of God church is incredibly conservative, and doesn't allow for the drinking of alcohol at all. That was the church I was brought up in, the church to which my father was so devoted. As I cracked open a can of beer, I thought, "Good. I *should* drink beer, and smoke pot, and maybe even do LSD. And get into fights. And who knows what else?"

After the party died down, I stayed and talked to Rich about how messed up everything felt in my home. I hated going to church, I explained, and I resented being forced to live under my parents' strict rules when it didn't even seem like they cared about me. The absolute worst part of my home life was just feeling alone and ignored, which is probably why my friends became so important to me. Friends are great, but nothing can take the place of parents who are there for you.

But as I was walking home, the guilt started hitting me. I didn't feel like this bad kid I'd become was truly who I was. I didn't want to be bad my whole life.

I wanted more than just my dad's attention, I soon realized. I wanted him to be proud of me.

———

I was in such full-blown teen angst at this time that I had no idea things were not exactly going swimmingly for my father, either. It's not easy to be in charge of anything, much less an organization like an Assemblies of God church. Everyone had their own opinions about the way the church should be run, and it turned out that while I was running around with my friends, sinning at every possible opportunity, my father was facing the doubts of the other church leaders.

After a while, I started to hear things: rumors, rumblings, whatever you want to call it. Since I was a kid, I was never told exactly what was going on, so all knowledge of what happened next, I received secondhand. But from what I can gather, there was a lot of internal conflict among the church leadership, and a lot of that had to do with my father. There was a member of the church who wanted to be a board member, but who was not qualified. My father had to tell him that he was unqualified in front of the people in church that evening. As a result, they decided to figure out how to get rid of the pastor. This was all because my father cared about the church and held the man accountable. They wanted to figure out how to get rid of the pastor. Because my dad held him accountable. With the Assemblies of God, it was all about swelling the numbers. The exact reason that they objected to him, I may never know. But what I do know is that as time went on, the rumblings became louder and louder.

And then one night, it all imploded.

It was a Wednesday night, and as I said earlier, that meant church for us. On this particular night, I was sitting, bored out of my mind, through a youth group meeting in the basement of the church. My father was upstairs with the parents and other church leaders in the auditorium.

The youth group was led by the youth minister, a nice enough guy named Rob. Rob had a wife and two kids, and I think he was a dentist when he wasn't teaching our sessions. But he seemed a bit younger and hipper than most of the other church parents, which might be why he was chosen for that position. Rob always made a valiant attempt to be entertaining during these meetings, but the cheese factor was high and it was hard to take him seriously. And since he was so earnest in his delivery, a lot of time was spent actively trying to suppress my desire to make fun of him. It didn't help that these youth functions were always tedious, with Rob telling us how to live right in accordance with God's will and such. Sometimes we'd play games in order to get us to interact, but they were always boring.

On this particular night, the youth group session included a lesson that still angers me to this day. There were about fifteen of us kids in the room, trying to stay awake as Rob droned on and on to us about friendship.

"The only real friends you'll ever make," he said, with complete and utter sincerity, "are the ones you meet right here at church. These are the friends who will be there for you, no matter what it is you need, no matter how low you may have fallen. They'll pick you up when you need to be picked up, or talk you down when you need to be talked down. But you see, people who *aren't* Christians... they'll never be there for you in times like that."

I rolled my eyes so hard I almost gave myself an aneurism.

He went on. "It's like that song 'Looking for Love in All the Wrong Places.' You guys know that song?" He looked around the room at each one of us, an expectant smile on his face.

If you're not familiar with it, "Looking for Love in All the Wrong Places" is a country song by an artist named Johnny Lee, and was featured in the movie *Urban Cowboy* with John Travolta.

I glanced around the room and saw some of the other kids vaguely nodding, which encouraged Rob to keep going. "Well, it's kind of like that. You need to look in the right place for love and friendship. And church is the *only* right place. It's only here where you'll make real friendships and connections with other people that you can depend on. Trying to forge these connections anywhere else will lead you down a path you don't want to be on. Believe me, guys."

I didn't believe him. In fact, I had to force myself not to stand up and shout at him. He was just so *wrong*. He had no clue what he was talking about. My friend Rich wasn't a Christian, I didn't meet him at church, and yet when a kid was shouting around the school that he was going to kick my butt, Rich defended me and put a stop to that real fast. That was real friendship, and it had nothing to do with the church whatsoever.

Rob went on, but I tuned him out, grumbling inside about the pointlessness of these meetings.

Eventually, mercifully, the youth service ended. All of us kids went upstairs to meet up with our parents, who were supposed to be ending their meeting in the auditorium at the same time. When we got upstairs, we saw through a window that all the adults were still in the auditorium, and several of them were gesticulating pretty wildly with their arms.

That's weird, I thought.

No one knew what to do, so we just kind of watched as the parents kept arguing. Some of the kids were trying to listen through the window, so I did, too.

"What are they saying?" someone asked.

"I'm not sure," I said. My curiosity was now in overdrive.

I struggled to hear what was being said, and was mostly unsuccessful. But then I managed to make out one of the adults asking, "What's the process of getting rid of a pastor?"

And then I knew something was very wrong.

We all watched the scene unfold, without hearing too much of the dialogue, and then eventually the parents started filing out of the auditorium. All of us kids did our best to pretend we hadn't been trying to eavesdrop.

As we were driving home, I was too nervous to ask my dad what happened in his meeting, so we just drove along in an incredibly uncomfortable silence. The next night, my parents announced we were going to be moving to a town called Moosic, which was four and a half hours away from Jeannette.

"*What?*" I said, shocked.

I felt my whole world falling apart around me. Sure, I was no stranger to moving, but this time it was different. This time I had friends, a group of guys that listened to me and were there for me and kicked people's butts for me if it came to that. I hadn't met them at church, but they were real friends, no matter what phony tale Rob had been trying to sell us.

The thought of leaving them made me insane.

"Why?" I asked.

My dad shrugged. "It's just a better opportunity," he said.

I felt a fury rise in me. I knew it was because the other people at church wanted him gone, and he was refusing to admit it.

"*How* is it a better opportunity?" I persisted.

"It's what God wants," my dad said, his voice completely neutral and unaffected. "So that's what we're going to do."

And that was that. In the church, playing the "God card" happened all the time, because it's a great way to end a conversation you don't want to be a part of. And my dad had just used it to explain why he was ripping me away from my friends, my life, and the town I'd called home for four years, which felt like an eternity to me considering how often we moved.

The next morning, I awoke, still in shock about the news. I talked to my mother about it.

"Why can't we just stay here?" I asked.

My mom didn't look me in the eye, but responded, "This will be a fresh start for you, John."

At some point over the night, their story had shifted. When I went to bed, the move was happening simply because it was God's will.

Now that the morning had come, it was my fault.

They were trying to spin the move as something they were doing for *me*. Me, the bad kid who gets into fights at school and drinks beers with his friends and doesn't go to church on Halloween. As if moving to another city would have somehow suddenly transformed me into a model Christian kid who always did his homework and never got into trouble.

And this yarn was cooked up simply to cover the fact that the real reason we were leaving was because of my father. He hadn't meshed well with the other church leaders, so now I was paying the price.

The audacity of this lie made me seethe, but what could I do? I was sixteen years old and dependent on them for everything. It wasn't like I could strike out on my own. So I swallowed my anger and said nothing.

As I went to school that day, I felt weighed down by an extreme sadness. My time in Jeannette was the first time in my life I'd been happy, and now it was being ripped away from me, and my parents didn't even care. And to make it worse, I knew that once we moved, there would be no more talking about Jeannette. It would be stricken from the record. Anything considered even remotely negative was ignored in our house, because my parents found that so much easier than actually dealing with problems.

And here's the crazy thing. Even though I knew all this, even though I knew everything was going badly and none of it was my fault, I still just bit my lip and went with it.

Because I wanted my father's approval. And I had no way of knowing this at the time, but it turned out I would go to extreme lengths to get it.

CHAPTER 2

My Calling

Riverside High, the school I went to after moving to Moosic, could not have been more different than the one in Jeannette. For one thing, the majority of the student body was white, and even though I'm white myself, it took some adjusting. When I had first got to Jeannette, I was harassed and picked on, threatened with beatings so many times before finally fighting Darnell and finding my group of friends. In Taylor, the bullying and harassing wasn't physical, but it was still here.

The snooty looks. The sideways glances. Kids at that school picked on me because, to them, I didn't belong there. I wasn't raised in that community, and I was far too rough around the edges to fit in. For a while, I attempted to make friends, but it soon became clear no one at the school wanted anything to do with me.

So I just figured, oh well, screw it, basically. If they weren't interesting in hanging out with me, I might as well get a job, and that way I could spend my time making some money.

While trying to bury how much I was missing Rich and the guys back in Jeannette, I searched for jobs that I figured I—as a high school junior with no work experience—could handle. I soon landed as an employee at the local Burger King, which to my surprise ended up being a really great and positive experience.

For one thing, there was my manager, Donna. She was a great, big Italian woman with a loud voice and warm smile. She was quick to laugh and I just loved her right away. From the minute she hired me, she let me know that she saw me as more of a peer and a coworker than some potentially irresponsible kid.

She was an enthusiastic and supportive manager, and she actually believed I was smart and capable, which was something I never heard at home. So those words coming from an adult meant a great deal to me. In fact, I so preferred Donna's company to that of pretty much any other adult in my life that I started working at the Burger King as much as the law would allow. I let her know that if anyone called out sick, she should call me right away and I would fill in their shift. Basically, because she treated me like a responsible employee, that's exactly what I strove to become for her.

That's not to say there weren't a few missteps, though. Shortly after starting work there, I got to be friendly with one of my coworkers, a kid named Bobby.

That was a big deal, considering I spent a lot of my junior year feeling pretty lonely and friendless. The Burger King was located in a town called Old Forge, and it was a popular place for high school kids to hang out, walking around or cruising the streets in cars with their friends. Seeing the kids move in their packs made me miss my friends back in Jeannette a lot, and I would get furious all over again that my parents pulled me out of a place where I was finally happy.

But working at the Burger King, suddenly I was around kids my own age for hours, and eventually I got be close to some of them, like Bobby. Excited to have a friend my own age, I was more than happy to hang out with him when he asked what I was up to one weekend. The only problem was Bobby was scheduled to work.

Since there wasn't enough time for him to find a replacement, we hatched a plan that he was just going to call in sick at the last minute. And for some reason that I can only chalk up to childish stupidity, I completely forget my filling-in deal with Donna.

As I wasn't scheduled for that night, I was thinking Bobby and I would be free to hang out. So Bobby came over to my place, and about an hour before his shift, he used our phone to call in. (Remember, this was the time before anyone had Caller ID, let alone cell phones, so Donna would have no way of knowing he wasn't calling from his own home.)

After the call, Bobby came back into the living room.

"How'd it go?" I asked.

"Not bad," he replied. "She said she understood, and hoped I got better soon."

A stab of guilt hit me suddenly. Donna was the first adult in my life I actually liked and respected, and I was complicit in lying to her. I thought about her there at Burger King, unexpectedly understaffed. Would she have to run around like crazy all night? Would she have to stay late?

As these thoughts swirled in my head, our phone rang. We rarely got calls on Friday night, so confused, I picked it up.

"Hello?"

"Hi, John, it's Donna."

I felt my pulse suddenly quicken. Of course! What was I thinking?

"Oh," I said. "Hi, Donna." I looked at Bobby, whose eyes widened.

"How's your night going?"

"Um... it's good."

And it was then I realized the folly in our plan.

Crap! I thought. *I should never have picked up the phone. And I can't even say I'm busy, because she knows I'm home.*

"Listen, Bobby just called in sick to his shift, so I'm going to need you to come in and fill in with him."

"Oh, uh..." I stammered, trying to come up with an excuse on the spot as to why I couldn't come in to work.

She then said, "And since he's standing right there next to you, I figure he'll be okay with you taking his shift."

I froze. "Wait, what?"

And then she laughed.

Oh, she knew. She knew the entire time what our plan was. How, I have no idea. But she did.

And here's the thing. Rather than confront us about it at work, she let us just go ahead with the dumb teenage plot anyway, and then got the last laugh when she triumphantly called us on our trick.

And you better believe I went in and covered Bobby's shift, my face burning red the whole time.

The thing is, that's such a significant episode in my young life because it was the first time an adult had caught me in a breach of proper behavior, and rather than freak out, she was somehow cool about it while also laying down the law. She knew kids could occasionally falter, and she never held any kind of grudge about it. With my parents and the teachers in school, any misbehavior was treated with stern rebukes and punishment. So for Donna to do this made me like and admire her even more than I already did.

And you better believe I never tried that trick again.

After a while, I began to think of the crew at Burger King as a little family. Donna was like a second mother to me, and I became tight not just with Bobby but his sister, Nikki, who also started working there, as well as another girl named Lori. None of them went to the same school as me, so Burger King quickly became the center of my social universe. I had more fun at work than I ever did at home, and certainly at school. Work kept me out of trouble, too.

Well, for the most part. I still smoked pot occasionally with Bobby and a few other kids, but I was officially retired from the father-shoving business, so that was a step up, at least.

The best part about the job, of course, was that I now actually had money of my own. An elderly woman in my congregation passed away during this time, and after her death her husband, Veto, was looking to sell her car. When I saw it, I knew I wanted it. It was a dark green 1981 Oldsmobile Omega. My dad gave Veto a computer for the car. Veto cut me a nice deal, and very shortly after, the car was mine.

The only other thing I took any joy in was the youth group I attended on Wednesday nights. The group wasn't part of the Assemblies of God church where my father worked—since I was the only teenager in that entire congregation, I went to a nearby group at a neighboring church in Clarks Green. And unlike the unsatisfying sessions I had with Rob back in Jeannette, I actually enjoyed going to the youth group in Clarks Green, for two main reasons.

For one, there were cute girls my age there. A *lot* of cute girls. And that was a perk I definitely never had back in Jeannette.

The other reason I liked going was the youth pastor who ran the meetings, a guy named Dan. Unlike his predecessor from my old group, Dan was actually a really cool and relatable pastor who never tried too hard to be friends with us. He just let it happen naturally.

I think because I was the odd man out, being the only kid from a different church, Dan paid extra attention to me and made sure I always felt included. A couple of times, he even took me golfing at a club he belonged to. One time, after a round of golf, we were eating lunch at the clubhouse and his eyes kept drifting to a table next to us.

"What do you keep looking at?" I asked him.

"Those people at that table are leaving, I think," he said in a whisper.

"So?"

"So," he said, "they're leaving a full basket of hot wings. They didn't even touch them."

I turned and saw the last of the diners taking their coats and walking away. And sure enough, there was a full basket of wings on the table.

"Cover me," Dan said. "I'm going in!"

With one quick motion, he leaned over and scooped up the basket, bringing it back to our table and setting it down.

As he dug into the first wing, I cracked up. I'd liked him before, but after that he had my utmost respect.

As my junior year continued, I found myself realizing something that was kind of a surprise to me. I'd enjoyed the youth group because of Dan and the cute girls who actually paid attention to me, but after a while I started to think about actually having a relationship with God and Jesus on my own terms. I know that sounds a little surprising, but it's the truth. The more I thought about it, and the more youth group sessions I attended, the more I started to think maybe that really was a good path for me. After all, while I'd reveled in fighting and drinking and doing drugs with Rich and the guys back in Jeannette, it had never really gotten me anywhere. Sure, I'd had a group of friends for the first time, but it hadn't exactly made me a better person, and it certainly hadn't made my dad pay any more attention to me.

So maybe I'll try this, I thought.

As it neared the end of my junior year, Dan suggested something to me that helped in further steeling my resolve to dedicate my life to God.

"There's this thing happening," he said one day. "With your church actually. Assemblies of God. It's a Fine Arts competition. Kids in youth groups from all over are coming together, and there's going to be a lot of singers, dancers, that kind of thing. But there's also a sermon category in the competition. The sermons aren't supposed to be long—only about five minutes or so. I was thinking... how about you give it a shot?"

"Me?" I asked.

"Yeah!" Dan said. "You've been growing a lot this year, spiritually. I think you'll get a lot out of it. Besides, people like listening to you. You'll be a natural."

The thought that anyone would be interested in what I had to say was still brand-new to me, and I'll admit, it was an exciting one.

"That sounds cool," I said.

"It is!" Dan said. "If you do end up doing it, then we'll have to come up with what your sermon is going to be about, but that shouldn't be too hard. I think you'll really get something out of this."

"When is the competition?"

"It starts early next year, so we have the summer to figure out what your sermon will be. And practice. A lot of practicing."

"Okay. Can I think about it?"

"Yeah, of course. But I'm going to nag you about it until you decide to do it."

I laughed. "Okay."

As the summer began, I did find myself spending a lot of time thinking about the possibility of delivering a sermon. I was sure that would make my dad happy, at any rate.

My father also helped me to develop a short sermon. He was able to get me scheduled to share my sermon with a few other churches. It was during this process that I realized how wrong I had been about my dad. I realized that my dad was always there for me. He may have missed a few things, but he was there when it counted and he made me feel good. For example, even though he missed some fishing trips, when he did go fishing with me, I felt like I was on top of the world. Also, my dad and mom would frequently eat at Burger King when I worked there just to show their support of me. In addition, my dad helped me get my first car, the 1981 Oldsmobile Omega. He also helped me get the car fixed up.

A few years earlier, my dad chose to take me to the Ford dealership when he bought a 1988 5.0 liter V-8 silver Ford Thunderbird. It was great to be with my dad doing those things together.

I also realize how blessed I am to have a godly father and mother. Even during my rebellious teen years, my dad still showed me his love in tangible ways. For example, I wanted a leather jacket since it was the "in" thing to wear. You would think he would tell me no because I was rebellious, but nope, not my dad. He decided to take me out to look for a leather jacket. It wasn't the leather jacket that that I loved the most; it was being with my dad and doing something together. It didn't matter what it was, it was just good to be with my father.

But then something happened that took my mind far from anything church-related.

I was working a shift as usual at Burger King when Lori, one of the kids I worked with, was going to bring in her friend to start working there as well, whose name was, as it turned out, Laurie.

"Lori and Laurie," I said when she told me.

"Our names are spelled differently," she said.

"But they sound the same. How will we know which one Donna's calling for?"

"I guess we'll just have to try and figure it out."

I laughed.

When Lori came in for that shift, Laurie was walking behind her. I couldn't see her at first, but then Lori moved out of the way, and then...

WHAM.

The moment I saw her, I couldn't take my eyes off of her. She was the most beautiful thing I had ever seen in my life, and it felt like time slowed down as she walked inside. Lori pointed her towards Donna's office, and I watched her go, mouth open, unable to look anywhere but at her. She had such beautiful eyes and a pretty smile, and her long, wavy blond hair bounced behind her as she moved. I found myself thinking she was probably the only girl in the world who could make a Burger King uniform look nice.

When Laurie went into Donna's office, I immediately started grilling Lori about her.

"How long have you been friends? What kind of music does she listen to? What does she like to do?" I said, all in a rush.

"Jesus, calm down," Lori said, smirking. "Umm... friends since elementary school, country music, and going to the mall and camping."

I wanted to ask her more, but she was called away to work the drive-through window, so I was left alone with my thoughts.

What was Laurie like? What did her voice sound like? Would she like me? Did I have anything to offer?

I mean, hey, I had a car. That's a start, right?

Eventually, Donna came out of her office with Laurie in tow, and she addressed us all. "Hey, guys," she said "This is Laurie, our newest hire. Everyone be nice and show her the ropes, okay?"

"Okay," we all said.

"Great," she said. "Laurie, I'll let these guys introduce themselves. Let me know if you need anything."

With that, Donna went back into her office, and Laurie looked around, a little unsure of what to do next.

This was my chance.

"Hi," I said. "I'm John."

She looked at me and smiled, and I felt a heat surge from my chest through my neck and into my face.

"Hi, John," she said. "I'm Laurie."

"Yeah, I know," I said, and we both laughed.

We were off to a good start.

At some point later in the shift, I was again alone with Lori, and I used that opportunity to ask the one question I was burning up inside to ask.

"So, uh, Lori," I said, trying my hardest to sound casual. "The other Laurie, is she, um... I mean... is she... does she have a boyfriend? Or anything?"

Lori smirked and shook her head. "Nope," she said. "She's single. Why?"

I wasn't making eye contact with her, but I could feel her eyes boring into me. Teenage girls could be terrifying when they wanted to be.

"No reason," I said.

"Uh-huh," she responded.

Over the course of the next week, I worked as many shifts as humanly (and legally) possible, eager to be around Laurie as much as possible. During that time I discovered she was more than just beautiful—she was kind and sweet-natured, intelligent and compassionate.

And, like I said, the fact she could make a Burger King uniform look attractive spoke volumes.

I desperately wanted to ask her out, but there was a problem—I'd never asked a girl out on a date before. Ever. In my life. Not even in kindergarten. Just the thought of it filled me with anxiety and made my palms sweat. The thought of her saying no, of rejecting me, filled me with fear and a dark despair. Maybe she didn't even like me at all. Maybe she was just tolerating me because we worked together and she didn't want to make it weird!

Get a grip, I told myself. *Just ask her out. If she says no, it'll suck, but it won't mean the entire world is ending. You'll survive.*

One Saturday, we both had a morning shift, and I thought, *This is it. It's now or never.*

I approached her as she was lowering a basket of fries into scalding hot oil.

"Hey, Laurie," I said, praying my voice wouldn't squeak or something equally embarrassing.

Fortunately, it didn't.

"Hey, John," she said, smiling her sweet smile. "What's up?"

"Yeah, um, listen," I said, trying to get through it as quickly as possible. "I was thinking, if you're not, like, you know, doing anything later this afternoon... do you maybe want to hang out at the mall with me?"

Her smile widened. She looked at me with those pretty eyes of hers and said, "Sure! That sounds really fun. I'd like that a lot."

"Great!" I said. "Awesome!"

"I'll need to go home and shower and stuff beforehand, 'cause... you know..." she said, motioning to her clothes and the fries. "Fast-food smell."

"No problem!" I said. "I can pick you up."

"Cool," she said.

"Aren't you supposed to be at the front register?" a voice behind me said.

It was, unmistakably, Donna.

I turned and laughed awkwardly, feeling my face flush. "Yep, going there now," I said.

"Mm-hmm," Donna said, a knowing smile on her face. "I thought maybe you got lost."

"Nope! All good."

I walked rapidly to the front register where a line of ornery-looking customers had formed and began taking orders.

The shift passed at a glacial pace. All I wanted to do was get home, shower, change, and hop back in my car and get on the date. It was probably the most excited I'd ever been up to that point. When at last the time came, I went to Laurie and excitedly told her I'd see her in a couple hours, then hopped in my car and headed home. As I was getting ready, my father asked me what my plans for the rest of the day were.

I told him I was going to the mall to hang out with a girl from work, hoping he wouldn't make it weird with any follow-up questions.

He did, but not in the way I expected.

"Where does she go to church?" he asked.

I hesitated.

"I don't know," I said. "I didn't ask."

My father frowned, and I knew that was a topic I should bring up later on the date.

I got in my car and picked up Laurie, and as I drove to the mall I kept thinking to myself how cool it was that this was really happening—I was on a date with the prettiest girl I'd ever seen in my very own car.

Not too shabby.

At the mall, we did what all kids did in malls in the 90s: roam around the outside of stores with no real direction, occasionally going in if something seemed interesting. Mostly, we spent the time talking. She told me all about herself, and kept asking me about my life. And when I told her, she really listened instead of just waiting for her turn to talk like most people do.

We had a great time, and at the end of the date I asked if she'd like to do it again some time, and she said yes. And then, just like that, boom. We were a couple. We would go out every weekend, to the mall or to the movies. Typical teenage boyfriend-girlfriend stuff.

Things were going pretty well for me. I had a job I liked with friendly coworkers, I had a girlfriend for the first time in my life, and to make things even better, I was actually enjoying going to church youth group. I guess you could say I really was on a spiritual journey, especially once Dan planted the seed of me delivering a sermon in the upcoming competition.

Because of my embracing of the church, I happily agreed to go on a spiritual retreat when my father suggested it. Sure, I was in no hurry to leave Laurie, but it was only for a week, and she understood.

The retreat took place at the Potomac District Youth Camp, back in Virginia near where we used to live. When I got there, I was excited to see so many kids my age in the same situation I was, and I felt close to a lot of them before too long. The speaker for the retreat was a pastor named Greg Hubbard, a charismatic evangelist who got us all fired up by talking about living our lives for God.

As he was speaking those words, I really felt something move within me. It's strange to look back on it now, but I really did. He encouraged us to go on our own and pray to God, to ask him what our true path in life would be.

So I did. I prayed. I remember praying with all my might, thinking, *I don't know what I'm supposed to do, or why I'm here. But I know I want to help people.*

And though it's hard for me now to remember the feeling, at the time I really did feel like a voice inside me said, "Okay, then that's what you'll do."

And just like that, I saw what my future held.

Like my father, I would be a pastor for the Assemblies of God.

Emboldened with this new calling, I was excited to talk to the other kids, and found a lot of them were feeling the same way. I'd never felt like this before, never felt like I belonged in such a specific way. One night there was a late-night snack social kind of thing where we were all hanging out without too much structure, and there I met two girls, a little older than me, both of whom attended Southeastern University, which is a Christian college affiliated with the Assemblies of God and located in Lakeland, Florida. We chatted for a bit and talked about Greg Hubbard's sermon earlier in the day, and I told them I prayed to God and heard him tell me I'm meant to be a pastor.

"That's great!" one of them said.

"You should think about coming to Southeastern," the other added.

"You think?" I said.

I hadn't really spent a lot of time thinking about where I would go to college once high school ended, but from the way they talked about it, it sounded like the perfect place for me to land. A school connected to the Assemblies of God, so my parents would approve. It had young, energetic professors who the girls said were inspiring to listen to. And hey, it was in Florida! I was no dummy. The Florida environment pretty much trumps Pennsylvania on every conceivable level. Who *wouldn't* want to go there?

"Definitely," one of them said. "You have to apply."

"Yeah," the other chimed in.

Without having to think about it too hard, I said, "I think I will."

So just like that, I knew my life's purpose and where I wanted to go for the four years after high school. Not bad for a week's time.

When I got back home, I realized the only flaw in my plan: if I did get accepted to Southeastern, it meant I would be a nineteen-hour drive away from Laurie.

But before that became an issue, I'd have to actually get in, not to mention I had all of my senior year ahead of me.

I hadn't liked anything about school when I transferred to Riverside High, and senior year didn't change anything about that. The only thing that made my time at school tolerable was knowing it was going to come to an end. I was still enjoying going to youth group and working at Burger King, and to my satisfaction, my dad actually seemed enthusiastic about my wanting to go to Southeastern and follow in his footsteps.

"I think this is a confirmation," he told me after I mentioned my experience at the retreat.

"What does that mean?" I asked him.

"A confirmation is a sign from God. It's when good things happen to you that let you know you're on the right path."

I liked the sound of that. A confirmation. Like when I decided I wanted to be a pastor, and then immediately met the girls who suggested going to Southeastern. It made sense.

There was still a huge problem between my father and me, though.

And that problem had to do with Laurie.

I brought her over to the house for the first time and introduced her to my parents, and after she'd left I was excited to see how my father would feel about her. I realize now I was stupid to expect him to have been supportive in any way.

He frowned after she left, and said, "She's just not ministry material."

I couldn't believe it. She and her family went to church all the time.

"Because she's a Baptist?" I asked.

"No, that's not it," my dad answered. "You're going to be a minister. Ministers' wives are expected to be proactive, to lead groups and charity functions and that kind of thing."

I couldn't believe it, and had to bite my lip to keep from shouting at him. How could he know what kind of wife she would be? We were teenagers! And he had only met her for a few hours. It was ridiculous.

But my dad's mind was made up. He decided that Laurie wasn't ministry material, and therefore she was nothing but a distraction and a waste of my time. And once his mind was made up, there was no changing it. After that, any time her name was brought up, he would show his disapproval.

A month or two after I had her over, I bought her a ring with her birthstone embedded in it. It was about a hundred bucks, which was maybe a little extravagant for a high school student, but I'd been working consistently for almost a year at that point and had saved up a good deal. My father, however, was outraged.

"You spent *one hundred dollars* on that? What were you thinking?"

"It's my money!" I replied, seething.

"Money you just wasted." He walked away in disgust, and it took every ounce of willpower I had not to follow him in the next room and continue the argument.

He was doing everything he could think of in order to drive a wedge between Laurie and me, but all he was actually doing was pushing me further away from him and our family and closer to hers. Laurie's parents were warm and kind, just like her, and unlike my dad, they approved wholeheartedly of our relationship. They would have me over for dinner and talk to me all about school and work and my desire to be a pastor. When I asked if Laurie could come with me to an Assemblies of God Youth Convention, which was an overnight trip—with thousands of other teenagers—they allowed it, because they trusted me. They even did something pretty amazing—just like Rich and the gang had done for me back in Jeannette, Laurie and her parents starting attending my dad's church, Moosic Assembly of God. I thought that was such a huge and generous gesture, but my father was unimpressed.

Laurie's parents were fond of camping, and they often went for weekend camping trips. One time, they invited me, and I couldn't have been more excited to go. I loved the outdoors, and the thought of sharing an experience like that with Laurie sounded awesome. Her parents would be there to supervise and make sure we didn't get up to any teenage shenanigans, so I figured my dad would be fine with me going.

He wasn't.

"What do you mean I can't go?" I said when he told me.

"It's inappropriate," he responded.

"Inappropriate? Her parents are going to be there the whole time!"

He shrugged.

"But they let her come with me to the Assemblies of God Youth Convention, and that was an overnight trip!"

"I gave you my answer, John."

And that was the end of it. There was no budging him.

When I told Laurie's parents about my dad's decision, I could tell they were angry at him, because it was a pretty blatant insult to their parenting skills. Did he think they were going to let us have sex in a tent or something? They were kind enough to try to hide from me how pissed off they were, but I could tell.

While all of this turmoil was happening with my father and Laurie, I was competing in the Fine Arts competition with my sermon, and to my surprise and delight, I was actually winning. The two things I was not at all accustomed to as a kid were winning and speaking in front of large groups of strangers, and now I was doing both. It was a pretty amazing feeling.

I won the penultimate competition in my division, in fact, and was invited to the Nationals in San Antonio, Texas. This was it. This would be the culmination of all of my hard work, and a way to show my father I was actually somebody important. I was so excited when I heard, and the first thing I did was head home and tell him.

"Well, we can't go to that, obviously," he said.

"*What?*"

It seemed like there was no end to his attempts to ruin my life.

"Why?" I asked, incredulous.

"We don't have the kind of money to take you to Texas," he said.

It was true, and I knew it. We weren't rolling in money, but we could have tried fundraising.

"That's money that should be going to your college fund. We're not going to waste it on a competition."

"A *sermon* competition!"

"It doesn't matter, John."

And it didn't matter. To him, anyway. He said we weren't going, so all of my hard work was for nothing. All the time I'd put in to developing that sermon, all the effort I'd made to overcome stage fright and learn how to speak in front of people, everything. It had all been a waste of time.

My senior year went on, and my life was basically Laurie and Burger King until at last my graduation ceremony rolled around, and then that was it. I had been accepted to Southeastern. I was now a high school grad, about to go off to college, knowing my life would never be the same.

And I was more than ready for it.

But the one thing I wasn't ready for was leaving Laurie. The summer after senior year felt mercilessly brief, as each day brought me one step closer to leaving her. It was agonizing, and then at last the moment arrived. The final night I spent with Laurie, I could practically feel my heart breaking. I knew we would talk all the time and see each other on breaks, but it wouldn't be the same, not by a long shot.

The next day, I said good-bye to my family. Then I kissed Laurie and was on my way to Florida and into a whole new life.

CHAPTER 3

College

Going from Pennsylvania to Florida was a heaping dose of culture shock to say the least, and I was glad for the familiarity of the church during this time. And it turned out I was about to receive another confirmation, the kind my dad had talked about after I'd come home from the Potomac Youth Camp.

"I wanted to ask you something," my student advisor said to me while I was still settling into my new school routine.

"Okay," I said.

"I was looking at your application, and I see you wrote 'delivering sermons' in the special skills category.

"Oh," I said. "Yeah."

I explained to him what had happened: how I'd kept winning the sermon competition but wasn't able to attend the finals because of my father's decision that it was too expensive.

"Oh, what a shame," he said. "I'm sure you wanted to go."

"I did," I said. "A lot. It was a pretty big disappointment."

"Well," he said, "we can't go back in time, but we may be able to take a little of the sting of that off."

"How do you mean?"

"There's a scholarship that we award for outstanding student sermons, as it happens. Would you want to perform your sermon for some of the staff here?"

I was surprised, to say the least. "Uh, yeah! When?"

He gave me a date and place, and I went through my old notes for the next week, reacquainting myself with the sermon I'd written with Dan's and my dad's help. When my appointment came, I went to the hall where my advisor had told me to meet him and performed the sermon in front of a small panel of judges. When I was done, they thanked me and I left the room. The next day, I was informed that I'd won the scholarship.

I couldn't believe it! It turns out all the hard work I'd done the year before hadn't been for nothing. It actually made the financial strain of college a little easier on my parents.

But when I proudly told my father about my victory, I was met with indifference. All I wanted was to see some kind of pride from him in the things I accomplished, but even when they directly benefited him, I still didn't get that. What was I supposed to do? It was infuriating.

Laurie, on the other hand, was never afraid of expressing how proud she was of me.

"That's amazing!" she said. "Think about how many sermons they probably saw, and they chose you! You must be so excited."

"Definitely," I said.

We were talking on the little pay phone that was in my dorm common room. (This was before all dorms had phones in them, keep in mind, and *way* before all college students came to school with their own smartphones.) This was my ritual every night: finish my classes, do my homework, then march out into the common room with a mountain of quarters and call Laurie. I must have gone through hundreds of dollars in quarters that first semester. I missed her so much, and hearing her voice was such a comfort to me.

"So... any crazy college parties?" she asked. I could tell she was smiling.

"Nah," I said, and it was the truth. I was more interested in learning my craft as a pastor and staying true to Laurie than I was in any typical college shenanigans. I couldn't be more different than the kid I'd been at fifteen. But I liked this version of me way more.

"So you're really gonna come back up to visit next week?" she said. "I mean, you just got there."

"I know, but we have half a week off for fall break, and I can't stand not being with you."

"Awww," she said. "I feel the same way."

And so the following week, I did make the drive up, all nineteen hours, just so I could see her for a few days. And then I drove up again for Thanksgiving, and again for Christmas.

"It's freezing!" I said when I saw her in December, and she laughed.

"It's always freezing in December. It's winter!" she said.

"It's not freezing in Florida," I said, winking, and she rolled her eyes and laughed again.

"Well, if you're that cold, maybe I should give you your Christmas present early. Come on inside! My parents want to see you!"

I went with her into her home, happy to see her parents again. Laurie disappeared into her room while I talked with her parents about my new college life. They asked me all sorts of questions about what my classes were like, how was I making out in the dorms, if I was making friends, etc. It was kind of impossible to not realize they showed a lot more interest than my own parents.

When Laurie returned, she was holding a big package in Christmas wrapping paper, but it wasn't clean lines like a box. More just a kind of bundle-shape.

"What is that?" I asked, smiling.

"Your Christmas present, silly. Open it!"

I took it from her and ripped off the wrapping paper, and found myself holding an incredibly soft knit blanket.

"This is awesome," I said.

"Thanks! I made it for you."

"Wait—you *made* this?"

"Yep."

"You didn't buy it?"

"Nope!"

I looked at the blanket in my hands. It was so intricately woven and soft to the touch, and I knew it must have taken her hours upon hours upon hours to make something as perfect as this blanket.

"I... I don't know what to say. Thank you."

I slept underneath that blanket that night, and took it with me when I returned to college. Even though the last thing I needed in the muggy Florida weather was another blanket, it reminded me of her and never failed to make me smile every time I came back to my dorm and saw it.

The spring semester passed uneventfully, and before I knew it I was back in Pennsylvania for the summer break. I toyed with going back to work at Burger King, but I decided that would feel like a step backwards, and so I got a job working for Coca-Cola, basically switching out syrup tanks for restaurants, bars, businesses that sold fountain drinks, etc.

One day when I was at work, I happened to glance at my watch. It was the middle of a shift, and the driver I was with asked me why I needed to know the time. He was an older guy who'd been doing the job for a while, and went on a bit of a tirade, saying we clock in at seven in the morning and clock out at five in the evening, and said there was no reason to know the time until it was quitting time. Apparently there was some kind of friction between the management of the company and the union of workers at the time, and rather than work the traditional eight-hour workday, we were working two extra hours each day to get overtime as a way of sticking it to the management. I realized he thought I was checking to see if it was almost three, and he was making sure I had no plans of leaving before 5 p.m.

I didn't wear a watch to work again for the rest of the summer.

June turned into July, which pretty quickly became August, and before I knew it I was heading back to Florida again for my sophomore year of college. My second year as an undergrad wasn't too different from my first, except I knew I needed to be a bit more social and not spend all my time on studies and phone calls with Laurie. I found out there was an intramural basketball team, which sounded perfect for me—all the fun of playing the game without having to commit to a student athlete's schedule. I started doing that, and went to Daytona Beach a few times with some friends, but other than that it was same old, same old. College for me was never painful or even uncomfortable, but it was also never the greatest years of my life, either, the way I hear some people talk about it. I did fine in my courses, and I stayed out of trouble. Before too long, it was summer again.

My parents threw me a curveball earlier in the year, though, in that they were moving once again: this time to Brunswick,

Maryland. At this point I felt like they would never stop moving, and my time away from home had made me start to feel a bit more adult and independent. I didn't feel a particular need to live with them in Maryland for the summer, especially because it would be so far from Laurie, and thoughts of being reunited with her were what kept me going throughout the year. She and I had already talked about her applying to Southeastern, and sure enough, she was accepted. So now it just felt like a waiting game until we were together all the time.

When I told Laurie about my parents' move, she had an idea: her sister and brother-in-law, who lived just a few minutes away from her and her parents, had a pop-up trailer that they parked on the street. Everyone agreed it would be all right for me to live in the trailer for the summer.

Everyone, that is, except my parents. When I explained to them my summer plans, they were furious. They really let me have it, and tried everything they could to convince me to live with them. I was all too aware that my dad still didn't approve of Laurie, and while that hurt, I followed my heart. I lived just outside her house all summer, working a job in construction, and saving my money.

Because I was going to buy her an engagement ring.

The summer went on, and my parents continued to state their disapproval, but I tried to force myself to stop caring. I was going to be starting my new life as an engaged man, and I wasn't going to let them get me down.

One day at church, I ran into Veto, the man who'd sold me his late wife's car when I was in high school. I told Veto about my plans to propose to Laurie, and he asked me if I had the ring yet.

"Not yet," I said.

"Here's what you do," he said. "Go to my pal Jimmy's jewelry shop. Tell him Veto sent you."

A little background about Veto: when he was a younger man, he served some pretty significant jail time due to... let's say a tiny little misstep, where he counterfeited coins and sold them to collectors for obscene amounts of money. He wasn't working alone—there were about five men involved, and they made hundreds of thousands of dollars in this operation. When they were caught, Veto ended up taking the rap, covered for his friends, and served many years in prison.

The Jimmy in question was one of the men Veto had worked with in the counterfeiting racket, and since he hadn't spent any prison time, he owed Veto something big. Following Veto's directions, I went to the jewelry store. When I walked in, I saw an older man with long spiral curly hair so gelled it looked soaking wet, a full long mustache, and tinted sunglasses. He looked like a character out of a movie.

"Hi..." I said. "Jimmy?"

"Yeah."

"Uh... Veto sent me."

He smiled and invited me to follow him through a door that led to the back of the building. I soon found myself in a tiny office with a wooden desk. Jimmy went to the desk and pulled out a drawer, and when I looked inside, I saw it was full of diamonds and other jewelry.

"Take a look," he said. "When you see what you like, give me a number."

"What do you mean, a number?" I asked.

"Whatever you can afford," he said. "That'll be the price."

I looked at all the items in the drawer in wonder. I knew this opportunity would never come again, so I had to take full advantage of it. I picked up what I thought was the most beautiful diamond ring in the drawer and handed over a very small bit of cash. I didn't want to commit highway robbery on Jimmy, but I only had a construction worker's salary, and besides, I was pretty sure Jimmy had done a fair bit of highway robbery himself in the past, so I didn't mind shortchanging him a little.

When the time came to propose, I surprised myself with how nervous I was. I had it all planned out: we were going on a camping trip near the beach, and I figured what's more romantic than a proposal next to the ocean? So I put the ring box in my front pocket, and off we went. We sat down in the sand and had a great time, talking, kissing, looking at the waves. I felt the ring box in my pocket and knew I was so smooth—she had no idea what was about to happen. Finally, we got to a point in the conversation where I knew it was time. I stood up and she stood up with me, but then I dropped down on one knee, pulled the ring box out of my pocket, and opened it.

"Laurie," I said, "I love you. I love you and I want to spend the rest of my life with you."

"Oh, my God," she said. Tears started welling in her eyes. But then she started laughing.

"Why are you laughing?" I asked.

"I just... I saw the box in your pocket. I knew it was there this whole time."

"You did?"

"It was really noticeable," she said, laughing some more.

Turns out I wasn't so smooth after all. But it was funny, and I laughed, too. "I was waiting for the right moment," I said.

"I think you found it."

"Laurie..." I said. "Will you marry me?"

"Yes!"

And just like that, I was engaged. I slipped the ring onto her finger, and we kissed and stayed on the beach for a long time, just enjoying the moment together.

I had never been happier, and when my parents (predictably) voiced their disapproval, I tried to not even acknowledge it. I was legally an adult, I had a fiancée, I knew what career I wanted... and yet, despite all that, the lack of my father's approval still stung so deep.

Soon the summer ended, and it was time for me once again to return to school. Only this time would be different, because at last, at *long* last, Laurie was coming with me! She was starting her freshman year at Southeastern, and I finally felt complete while at school.

———

My junior year felt a lot more intensive than my first two, as my courses were getting harder and I was doing everything I could to become the perfect pastor. There was a preaching team on campus that I was determined to join, even though they had a rule of only taking seniors. I met with the team and pled my case, and as would be expected, they resisted at first.

"Let me just show you what I got," I insisted, and eventually they relented and allowed me to deliver my sermon—the same sermon that got me the scholarship to Southeastern in the first place.

When I was done, I was met with a few open mouths. Then finally, the captain of the team gave me the thumbs-up. "Okay, you're in," he said.

As I headed back to the dorms to tell Laurie the good news, I could barely contain my excitement. That minor victory was just one more confirmation—as my dad liked to say—that I was on the right path. I was on the God train, and it was exactly where I belonged.

I called my parents about getting onto the preaching team, and my dad was excited for me and actually praised my efforts, which surprised me and pleased me greatly. But there was still the nagging undercurrent of disappointment in his voice, because all my success was tainted, in his eyes, by the fact that I was engaged to Laurie. No matter what I did or said, no matter what *she* did or said, his mind was made up about her and he wouldn't budge. She could have walked on freaking water and revived Lazarus in front of his eyes and he'd still say she wasn't "pastor's wife material."

I wish I could say, looking back, that I was able to shrug off my dad's feelings towards Laurie, but the fact is, they ate me up inside. All my life, I so desperately wanted my father's approval, and the only hint of it I ever got came from my applying myself to follow in his footsteps. It was like being a starving man, surviving on tiny scraps of food thrown your way every once in a while, just often enough to keep you alive.

And in a desperate move for such survival, I did something that I have never forgiven myself for, and most likely never will.

It was a Sunday about halfway through my junior year. Laurie and I went to church, as we did each Sunday. The whole drive to church I knew what I was going to do, and yet even as the thoughts rolled around in my head, I couldn't believe they were there.

But they were.

I was going to end our engagement.

I went about it in the worst possible way, and there's no point in sugarcoating it, so this is how it happened:

In the middle of the pastor's sermon, I leaned over to Laurie and quietly whispered, "Can I see the engagement ring?" She looked confused, but took it off and handed it to me. I then put the ring in my pocket and told her, "We have to talk."

She went white as a ghost, and it was clear on her face she knew what was happening. She was far too classy to make a scene, so she silently stood up and walked out. Feeling more shame than I'd ever known, I followed her out.

I have no excuse for the way I handled this, but I can only say I was so indoctrinated by my upbringing I didn't even realize how horribly hurtful it was.

Laurie didn't wait for me in the lobby of the church, but went right to the car. As I slowly headed in the same direction, the youth pastor there stopped me. He was a guy named Eddy, and a real decent person. We knew him fairly well, and I could tell from the expression on his face he knew something was very, very wrong.

"What's going on?" he asked.

I showed him the ring, and it all clicked into place for him.

He then asked, "Do you want it to work?"

Miserably, I replied, "No."

"Then there's nothing I can do," he said. "I'm sorry, John."

He was right. If we were struggling through something but united in our desire to save our relationship, counseling from pastors could have been a great help. But the problem wasn't some external thing. It was me. I was bending to my father's will, and there was nothing to be done about it.

The ride home was silent and horrible. It was also forty minutes long, and when you're in that kind of situation, that's an eternity of torment. When we finally got back to campus, Laurie got out of the car, looked me dead in the eye, and said, "You're only doing this because of your father."

I couldn't bring myself to admit it. But we both knew the truth.

She turned and walked away, and that was it for us. The girl I met working at Burger King in high school... the first girl I ever loved... the girl I thought for sure I would marry... I just stood there and watched her walk away from me forever.

She was the love of my life. And then, just like that, she was gone.

In 1994 during the spring break of my junior year, I attempted a journey back home, but there were a few bumps in the road. It was a fourteen hour drive from Lakeland, Florida to Fredrick, Maryland. I needed to prepare my 1981 Oldsmobile Omega. I stocked up with snacks, mostly Combos and Reese's Peanut Butter Cups, and a copious amount of Mountain Dew. At sunset, I took off. I prefer to drive at night as there is less traffic and I feel it just provides a more peaceful trip. While I was making my way through North Carolina, my "Check Engine" light came on and there was a clunking coming from my engine. I pulled off at the closest exit to try to find a garage that would be open this late at night. Not surprisingly, none were open during the wee hours of the night. So, I headed to the local Waffle House pondering my options. There, I met a man who just so happened to be a tow truck driver and who also happened to know a mechanic. He helped me tow my car to the mechanics house so it would be there ready for him first thing in the morning. Then the tow driver took me back to the Waffle House to wait until morning. I got some quarters and headed to the pay phone. Anxiety began to build as I dialed my father's number. I pondered my options of how to handle the conversation, but either way it had to happen. So, I called to wake him up and fill him in on the situation.

"Hello?" my father said groggily.

"Hey, Dad. I'm sorry I woke you up."

"Are you okay? Are you in trouble? What's wrong? What do you need? Where are you?" his parental instincts immediately alert.

"Well, I'm stuck at the Rocky Mount exit in North Carolina." I went on to explain the entire situation and waited for his response.

"Well son, you stay put and I'll come down and get you." He replied without missing a beat.

My dad then made the five and half hour drive down to the Waffle House. When he arrived, it was still too early for the mechanic shop to be open. So, we sat and waited together. I was extremely thankful for his company and his willingness to come to my aid. After about an hour, the shop was open and things began rolling. We headed on over to hear the mechanics read on the situation and get it fixed. Turns out it was a minor issue which he fixed, but he left me another issue. While getting to work on my car, he had to cut all the air conditioning lines. However, he never connected them back. He apparently hadn't had his coffee yet. My dad and I decided that we would just deal with no air conditioning for the time being and then address that once we got back to Fredrick. My dad paid the mechanic his $500. I was extremely grateful for that as $500 for a college student is quite daunting. We thanked the man for his time, got in our separate vehicles, and headed home.

I'm still tremendously thankful for my dad coming to help me that day. It touched my heart that without hesitation, he jumped out of bed, made a long drive, sat with me, and helped me navigate the bump in the road. Even though we have our downs, I do rather cherish the ups and his love for me.

CHAPTER 4

A Tale of a Traveling Youth Minister

The rest of my college experience is one big blur, as all the classes and activities have blended together in my memory, and I didn't enjoy any of them. With Laurie no longer a part of my life, I did my best to find some semblance of meaning in other areas, but mostly came up empty.

I doubled down on my studies and graduated a semester early. I wanted to walk in my graduation ceremony, but my father said we didn't have money for my cap and gown nor was he able to take the trip to Florida to watch, so I ended up not attending. Once I finished my last exam, I got in my car and just drove to Maryland to live with my parents. Just like that, college was over and I was on to the next chapter in my life.

The previous summer, I'd started a children's ministry program at my dad's church working with kids up to the fifth grade, and so when I came back home I continued that program. My eldest brother, Pete, worked as the youth pastor, but despite the similarity in our jobs, we remained as close as we had been as kids, which is to say not at all. It's not that I didn't want to be close, but there was just so much tension between us. We were very different. I had creative and energetic ideas, often trying to think outside the box to improve our services. I would befriend some of the youth as a way to get to know their families. Pete was more like my dad, in that he was very conservative, and our philosophies just didn't mesh.

I knew, of course, this was a temporary position for me, as I had no wish to live with my parents for any extended period of time. I wanted to feel like an adult, and strike out on my own, so I started to put out feelers for jobs at other churches.

The Assemblies of God churches are all independent from one another, so there's no sort of centralized job listings or anything like that. Positions were usually heard about through word of mouth. Through the grapevine, I heard about a job opening up at a church in South Carolina, and since it meant doing youth and children's pastoring, I applied. I was thrilled when I was offered the position, feeling like I was finally on my way to being an adult—a job of my own not in my dad's church, and living by myself in a new state. I was excited for it, and became even more so when I negotiated my pay from the original $16,000 offered up to $20,000. My dad didn't want to see me going to my first church job with the Oldsmobile Omega so he gave me his 1988 5.0 liter V8 Ford Thunderbird as a gift before my first job.

But it turns out I shouldn't have been so excited.

If my dad was strict, the head pastor of this church, a man named Chuck, was a one-man authoritarian regime. My dad looked warm and fuzzy next to him. Chuck lived his life by the motto that you work like it all depends on you, and pray like it all depends on God. Sick days were unheard of, and vacation was a mythical thing only to be found in the realm of fiction.

I bristled under his ultraconservative directives, but I did my best to fit in. After all, this was my first time up at bat as a grown man working in the world, and I wanted to excel. I wanted to fit into his system, never take time off, never get sick...

... and then I had to get an emergency appendectomy.

I was at work when I started feeling intensely sharp pains in my stomach, to the point where I thought I might black out. I didn't want to admit it to anyone, but eventually they got so bad I had no choice, and I told the church's secretary I was going to the hospital.

I was put into the operating room almost immediately. When I was recovering, I was surprised when Chuck showed up in my recovery room. I tried to joke with him, saying, "I hope this is okay," meaning I hoped it was acceptable to be excused from work when undergoing a lifesaving procedure.

He was not amused.

The surgeon who worked on me told me to take a couple weeks to recover, but when I mentioned that to Chuck, he wouldn't hear of it.

Three days later, I was back at work, delivering a sermon for a children's service.

That's just how life was at this particular church. And at twenty-two, I was way too young to know when to speak up for myself.

I threw myself into work, and tried to forge a real bond with the kids in my charge, which unfortunately ended up being my downfall. After six months working at this church, I was called into Chuck's office. There were two other church officials with him, and I knew immediately this wasn't a good sign. At first I thought being called in was like being sent to the principal's office in high school. But once I got there, it felt more like being dragged into a police interrogation room.

"What's going on?" I asked.

Chuck folded his hands and stared me down.

"There's no easy way to say this," he said. "There have been enough incidents on your record that I've found... troubling... that I needed to bring you in to talk to you."

"Incidents?" I said.

No one had mentioned anything to me.

Chuck had a piece of paper in front of him, and he looked down at it. "Some of your activities with the youths have raised some red flags. There was a... rock concert?" He looked up at me, frowning.

"You mean the Jars of Clay concert?" I asked. It was true—I'd taken some of the kids on a field trip to see Jars of Clay, and yes, they were technically a rock band.

A *Christian* rock band.

But that minor detail didn't permeate the acrid fog around Chuck.

"Jars of Clay..." he muttered, repeating me. He read the paper some more. "And I see you had a lock-in where you allowed the kids to watch an adult movie?"

"Excuse me?" I sputtered. I scanned my memory, trying to figure out what he could possibly be referring to. In my time there, I'd had only one lock-in, and the movie we watched was...

"*Independence Day*? Is that what you mean?"

He nodded. Apparently in his view, a PG-13 movie where Will Smith and Jeff Goldblum save the world from aliens qualified as an "adult movie."

"And lastly, someone reported you engaged in some very inappropriate anatomical humor with some of the boys at a function."

I did my best to not roll my eyes. There had been a youth function with a Ping-Pong table, and a bunch of rowdy sixteen-year-old boys were playing around on it. I'd made an innocent joke where "balls" had been a double entendre. Not exactly scandalous.

"Therefore," Chuck continued, "I'm sorry to say that your character doesn't seem fit for ministry. You're fired."

My eyes widened. "Are you serious?" I asked.

I couldn't believe it. I had put so much hard work into this job, even to the detriment of my own health, and I was being fired for no real reason other than the lead pastor didn't like me. It was outrageous. But churches were not exactly a democracy, and there was nowhere to go that I could plead my case. The lead pastor had the final say in all matters, and so that was it. I was out of a job.

Humiliated, I returned to my parents' house, feeling deeply ashamed and foolish. I thought my career was over before it even began, and I'd never be hired again.

Fired because of a flaw in my character? That's a damning statement, because it means I wasn't really fired for something I'd done. I'd been fired for *who I was*. How does someone recover from something like that?

Through some grace of the universe, I was able to secure another job at a different church. This one was in Page, Arizona, near the border of Utah. I was excited for this second chance, and the opportunity to rehabilitate my image. I would make sure to keep my more fun-loving tendencies in check. I'd be a model youth pastor, and would make sure to create a rich, healthy, spirited place for all the kids to come and find their faith, to really be there and commune with God...

The problem was, when I got there, there weren't any kids.

Well, not exactly. There were five kids. Two of which were the lead pastor's children.

I couldn't believe it when I got there. How had no one told me? I was used to working with dozens of kids, arranging events with the idea that the numbers would be high. I wasn't sure how I was going to work with just five kids.

But then I admonished myself for complaining. This was a job, when just weeks earlier I thought I'd be a pariah in the church community for life. This was an opportunity for a do-over, and I wasn't going to waste it.

The church had set up a living situation for me, which was... less than ideal. There was an older man who worked for the church named David, and he lived in a two-room mobile home. When I arrived at his trailer, bags in hand, I first saw him sitting and watching television.

"Hi!" I said. "I'm John."

He looked at me like I was a squashed bug on the bottom of his shoe. "Hi," he said.

And that was it.

That was pretty much what all of our conversations were like.

The town of Page was tiny and unexciting, with a population of only about six thousand people. It was hard to drum up anything too exciting for the kids, but I did what I could. One girl in my youth group was dating a Mormon boy who lived in the town, and he played in a band. I had the idea to have his band play at our church as part of an outreach program, and while it did draw in about a hundred and fifty kids, most of them were Mormons, meaning they weren't exactly looking to convert to our church any time soon. And finding converts was, in fact, the whole point of outreach programs.

While I desperately tried to prove the necessity of my position, my mind started to wander towards the idea of finding a life partner. I realized I was still punishing myself for the way

I ended my relationship with Laurie, and had a long talk with myself about it. I had done something awful—there's no question about that. But it had been a few years at this point, and I figured it was time to forgive myself. That doesn't mean letting myself off the hook, but rather learning from that experience so I wouldn't hurt another person in the same way ever again.

I became friendly with one of the girls who worked as a youth helper at the church, and after a few weeks of light flirting, I asked her out to dinner. I wanted to be discreet about it, mostly because I didn't want to deal with the rumor mill. The church atmosphere is incredibly small and incestuous, and it's virtually impossible to keep a secret for too long. It was inevitable that a relationship would be discovered eventually, so I wanted to keep everything low-key for as long as possible.

As it turned out, I didn't need to worry, because after I went to dinner with this girl, I knew there was zero chemistry. Same thing for the second girl I went out with. We went roller-skating, which I thought might make for more conversation, but no. There wasn't a click.

As the months ticked by, I saw the signs all around me that the church really didn't have a lot of money in its budget for... well, for much of anything. For example, we'd recently had an evangelist named Matt Roever come and perform revival services for two weeks. Matt was actually a friend and former classmate of mine at Southeastern, so when the time came to pay Matt for his services, the lead pastor, a man named Dave, asked me to do it.

"Why me?" I asked. Normally someone in his position would hand out the payments.

Embarrassed, Dave told me that the total offering that came in after two weeks of revival services was a mere sixty-two dollars.

After half a year, Dave told me he wanted to have a conversation that he felt just awful about. Before he said another word, I knew what was coming.

"It has nothing to do with you," he said. "Please understand that. I think your performance has been more than we could have ever hoped for. It's just that..."

"There are no kids," I said.

He nodded. "We can't really justify using the budget to pay for your position."

"I understand. I had an idea this was coming."

"But again, it's not you."

"It's okay," I said. "If there's no money, there's no money."

Another six months, another job had come to the end. Fortunately, I had a colleague that connected me with a job in a place called Fountain Hills, also in Arizona. Dave had said good things about my performance, and the word of mouth was passed along from church to church in my favor.

Fountain Hills couldn't have been more different than Page. The town was incredibly vibrant and affluent—a lot of money was allocated towards their very active children and youth programs. With all of those resources, I was in hog heaven. I dove into the job, doing everything I could to be the best youth pastor I could. I helped the kids create a band (with a full sound system). I organized parties, I set up events. I was on a roll.

At the time, there was a huge movement in the faith community called the Brownsville revival. Long story short, a Pentecostal church in Pensacola, Florida, began holding sermons and drawing in insane amounts of people, often in the tens of thousands. It's reported that over the five years the revival was in effect, over four million people came to Florida to pray for repentance and find God.

It started in 1995, and over the next few years just snowballed into a worldwide phenomenon. People came from all over the world to attend church in Pensacola. The lead pastor of my church, Stephen, grew obsessed with Brownsville, and started to model our church after their aesthetic. He would buy banners and dress the auditorium like Brownsville did, hoping we would rake in newcomers to the faith in a similar way to Brownsville.

His obsession with Brownsville culminated in him asking me to drive with two other church officials and a swath of kids to Pensacola to witness Brownsville firsthand. It was a thirty-one-hour drive both ways, and we drove it without stopping for the night so we could get the kids to see it.

I will say, even if you're not someone who's at all religiously inclined, it was a sight everyone should see, if only for the psychological study. People were throwing themselves on the ground, weeping in front of thousands of strangers, shaking and convulsing on the carpet... it was something, all right.

And let me tell you. As someone who *was* religiously inclined at the time, I was all in. The experience moved me in a way that was far different from any other sermon I'd ever seen. I loved it. And I wasn't the only one, either, as several of the teenagers that came on that trip were so moved that they gave their lives over to God right then and there. From that moment on, they were determined to work within the church and spread the word.

I was thrilled with how the experience was received, but Stephen was not. I realize now that he was an egomaniac who didn't want to give credit to anyone else for the enthusiasm of his congregation, but at the time, I thought I was doing something wrong. He was very cruel and standoffish with me, despite the effort I was putting in with my every waking hour. Nothing I could do was good enough for him.

Stephen had two twin daughters who were in my youth program, and both of them had what we call spiritual encounters during nights I led sermons for them. Not to sound boastful, but I was nailing it at my job and as such became well-liked within the congregation, and Stephen took that as a threat to his dominance. So one day, with no warning, he brought me into his office and said, "If I would have known who you were before I hired you, I never would have hired you."

I was stunned. "What does *that* mean?" I asked, my face getting hot.

"I think you know what it means," he said. "I'm sorry, but I'm afraid it's not working out. Your time with us is done. I want you to clean your office out immediately. And, if you speak of this to anyone, I will revoke your severance pay."

"Are you serious?" I asked. I was incredulous. I knew he was petty, but actually firing me for being more popular than him was a step beyond what I'd thought he was capable of.

"I'm very serious," he said.

I put my hands on the desk and leaned over, bringing my face close to his. I was pleased when he defensively backed up.

"You're an insecure idiot," I said.

Disgusted, I stalked out of the room. I went to my apartment and furiously threw my clothes into a bag, then stopped and made myself calm down a bit. I couldn't believe it, but again, I was let go after working for only six months. It had become a trend, after all.

Not knowing quite what to do, I called one of the board members with whom I was friendly and told him what happened. I asked him for a letter of recommendation, which he was more than happy to give me. I then called a couple board members and asked them to help me pack up my things. They were also kind enough to agree to help. After my Penske truck was all packed up, I handed the board members copies of the letter of recommendation. Needless to say, they were surprised at what happened.

I moved back to my mom and dad's house, feeling real beat up. I started thinking I would never have a real career, and wondering if I was even doing the right thing. *Maybe I'm not meant to be a pastor,* I would think. *Maybe I'm meant to walk a different path.*

I thought about going back to school and getting a degree in another field. But then I was contacted by a church in Columbus, Georgia, asking if I would join their pastoral staff. Hoping the fourth time would be the charm, I agreed to take the position, and moved once again.

As with the last job, I resolved to jump in with as much energy as I could possible summon. I wanted to hit the ground running, and so I immediately started going out into the community and started meeting people.

The first people I met were Jeff and Catherine. They were a young couple, recently out of the military, and just newly into God. They were curious and enthusiastic, and I befriended them very quickly. They asked me if I could come to their house and talk about God, teach them what I knew, that kind of thing. They were eager to learn, and so I would come over pretty regularly, Bible in hand, and talk to them about God's teachings. Seeing how into it they were reminded me of why I'd chosen this life in the first place, and I was grateful for them. I met them exactly when I needed to, and I hope they remember me in the same way.

One day, they asked me if I would talk to a friend of theirs, Paul. His life was a mess, and he was at a crossroads. If he took the wrong path, they were worried he would end up in a very dark place. So Paul came over one day, and I talked to him for a long time. I could tell he felt alone, but being there with me, and having Jeff and Catherine cheering him on, turned things around for him. He felt a sense of community, and started coming over to their house every time I did. This is one of the positive things I'll say about religion: it can give you a family when you need one the most.

One day, Paul was hanging out with Jeff and Catherine, and a Mexican man passed by their porch.

"Hey!" the man said to them. "You guys got any drugs?"

"No, man," Paul said. "We got something *better* than drugs."

They called me to come over, and not really sure what was happening, I did. While I was driving over, the three of them talked to the man, whose name was Richard, about how I was able to teach them about how God can turn their lives around. They were so earnest in their emotions that by the time I arrived, the hard work had already been done. Richard was ready to be saved.

So I just went with it, teaching Richard what he knew about Jesus. Richard was undocumented, and he was only planning to be in the area for two weeks. With the clock ticking, he was eager to be baptized and seal in his new faith.

"Can you baptize me this Sunday?" Richard asked.

"Of course," I said. "Let's do it."

I wanted to do something extra special for Richard's baptism, so Jeff, Paul, Catherine, and I put our heads together. It was Jeff and Catherine who came up with the perfect gift idea.

One of their favorite passages from the Bible was Matthew 17:20. In it, Jesus tells a man, "If you have faith as small as a mustard seed, you could say to this mountain, 'Move from here to there,' and it will move. Nothing will be impossible for you."

It's a beautiful, powerful passage, and particularly poignant for someone new to the faith. So we bought a brand-new Bible for Richard, and on the front we taped a tiny mustard seed, to represent the seed of his new faith. I baptized him that Sunday, and then the others presented him with the Bible. It was a beautiful moment that I'll always remember.

Jeff and Paul had the kind of energy a lot of people new to religion discover in themselves—an eagerness to help others while also helping themselves. One Friday night, they came to me and said they were going to a nearby Denny's at midnight to save as many people as they could. I thought that sounded a little on the sketchy side, but it was hard to shoot down their enthusiasm, so I went along with them. When we got to the Denny's, there were three tables full of young kids, all dressed from head to toe in full goth regalia. They looked like extras from a Marilyn Manson video. (Keep in mind, this was 1999.)

Ignoring the black lipstick and satanic symbols, each one of us took a table and started spreading the word to these kids. By the end of the night, even though I was unsuccessful with my table, Jeff and Paul had both managed to find kids that wanted to be saved. One minute they were scratching anarchy symbols into notebooks, and the next they were ready to read the Bible. It really was a remarkable thing to witness.

This fervor of my new friends spilled into the next project I worked on, which was an outreach party at a local high school called Jordan High. The principal of the school was a member of my church, and so I worked with him on coordinating the event, which turned out to be a smash hit. I invited a local alt rock band called Chrome Donuts to play, which obviously delighted the kids. In the school basketball court, we set up a $10,000 free throw competition. In addition to that, there was a host of other games with prizes, free pizzas, soda fountains, the works.

We also did a live performance that interpreted the Henry Rollins song "Liar," a song written from the perspective of the Devil. In this performance, Jeff played Satan, and Paul was in it as well. Catherine also spoke to the kids about the sexual and physical abuse she survived, and how her newly discovered faith in Jesus saved her from a life of despair.

Over six hundred people ended up attending, and the crowd was so large we were even covered by local news crew. In the end, fifty-five high school kids ended up signing up to be members of our church, which is almost a ten percent conversion rate, an impressive ratio for this kind of thing. It was a huge win for us, and I was extremely pleased.

I thought this was it—I'd finally truly found my stride, and had at last landed in the perfect job for me. I was riding high, and absolutely nothing could go wrong.

Until it did.

I was still single, and the pickings were pretty slim when it came to women. And I was a young man in my sexual prime with no real outlet. So I made a mistake, which is I allowed myself to get caught up in a sexy conversation with someone in an AOL chat room.

Again, remember... this was the 90s.

For some of you reading, this may be hard to wrap your head around, but working for the church means you're never not at work. So even though this sexy chat had nothing to do with my job at the church, it still held the gravest of consequences. Yes, the chat took place on my own personal computer. Yes, it was on my own time, when I was home. Yes, it was with a consenting adult. And yes, it was just a *chat*, meaning there were no raunchy pictures exchanged or anything like that. Just a simple, if perhaps racy, conversation that acknowledged basic human sexuality.

But when you work for the Assemblies of God, that means you can't conduct yourself in such a manner ever, no matter what.

So how did my superiors at the church even know about it, you ask? Well, it turned out the woman I was allegedly chatting with was in actuality the family member of someone in the church. It was a sting operation—someone had it out for me—and this person showed the transcript of the chat to the lead pastor. To this day, I still have no idea who it was.

The day after the chat happened, the lead pastor called me into his office, and I was starting to feel a sense of déjà vu when I sat down opposite him. He didn't mince words, bringing up the chat immediately. I was embarrassed, even though I knew I shouldn't have to be—everyone has sexual impulses, and it was ridiculous that the church was so strict about it. But being a pastor was the life I chose, and celibacy until marriage was part of it, so I had to make my peace with that idea.

There was no point in denying my actions considering he had evidence, so I told him the truth—that I had made a stupid choice in the heat of the moment. I apologized and promised not to do it again, and figured that would be that. I had been a model youth pastor and had brought so many people into the church, I thought there was no way he would seriously hold such a minor slipup against me. After all, who would shoot themselves in the foot by letting go the one person who'd turned so much around for the church, who was popular and respected and had brought so many new members into the fold? Who would possibly do something like that?

It turned out he would. He fired me on the spot.

I couldn't believe it. For the *fourth* time, I only lasted six months on a job before being let go. Sure, the second one had occurred because that particular church just couldn't afford to pay me anymore, but still. It was not a pattern anyone would want on their resume, and I really started to freak out about my future. I felt like something was wrong with me, something deep inside, something that was preventing me from keeping a job.

I couldn't bear the thought of moving in with my parents a third time, so instead I implored my brother Pete to let me live with him in Winchester, Virginia. It was only an hour away from my parents, but at least it was more of a buffer zone than a bedroom wall. My brother was still working with my Uncle Malcolm, and once I got back, I asked Malcolm if we could meet and talk about my career.

"What's going on?" Malcolm asked me.

"I don't know. I feel like there's just something not right about me. Why can't I hold down a job?"

Malcolm looked at me thoughtfully. "There could be any number of reasons. How long have you felt like it's your fault?"

I shrugged. "Kind of since the first job I lost."

"Well, if that's how you really feel, I think we should take some action."

"Like what?"

"We can have you evaluated at Emerge Ministry. See what they think."

Emerge Ministry is an entity that oversees the pastors who work for Assemblies of God churches, and I felt like if anyone could find out what was wrong with me, it would be them, so I went.

But after a week, they came up with nothing. No one could explain why I couldn't hold down a job.

Looking back on that time now, I realize that I was clearly going through a severe depression. I went through life with this feeling that something was always weighing me down—like a monkey on my back, I used to call it. No matter what I did or how hard I tried, something would always go wrong for me.

But the thing is, the world was different then. We didn't understand depression the way we do today—even today, there's a huge stigma about it. But at least we know depression exists now as a very serious diagnosis, which in the 90s was simply not part of the conversation. So I just went about my life, untreated for this debilitating illness.

In fact, the more I examine my life in detail, I realize I showed many signs of depression growing up, but I was so indoctrinated by the church that I pushed those feelings down deep and ignored all the warning signs. I put my faith in God, which is fine and I would never admonish anyone for that, but what would have helped me a lot more at the time would have been to also put my faith in science and the medical community. It would have done me a world of good.

After I returned from Emerge Ministry with a clean report, I had a long talk with Malcolm. He gave me a pep talk about believing in myself, and together we worked out what would be the next phase of my life. After giving it some thought, we concluded I should go to seminary school. Even though I hated the term "fresh start," because it took me back to my childhood when my mother would throw that term around every time we moved, that was how I looked at it. A fresh start. I'd tried jumping right into the professional field after college, but maybe my education wasn't totally complete after all. I could flush the last few years away and renew myself with studies. For the first time in a long time, I actually felt excited about something.

And so I enrolled in seminary school for the purposes of getting a Master's of Divinity. What I didn't know at the time, however, is that seminary school would do more than just more fully prepare me for the life of a pastor. It would in fact give me my life's new purpose, as well as introduce me to the woman who would become my wife.

CHAPTER 5

A Fresh Start

In the fall of 1999, I began my tenure at the Assemblies of God Theological Seminary in Springfield, Missouri. While I maintained my excitement about rebooting my life's journey, there was a bit of a feeling of going back in time. After all, I had lived the student life already, then graduated and set out into the world. So, to be a college student once again was a bit jarring, to say the least.

What's more, the seminary school was an incredibly socially conservative place, and I had a naturally rebellious streak that could never be defined as "conservative." I had always been the kind of pastor that threw parties and took kids to rock concerts and played pool with the church youth, which was not the description of a typical student in my new school.

But still, I liked the idea of seminary school, because it meant, to me, that I would gain a stronger foundation in my faith. I thought it would elevate not only me but the people around me, and the discourse I shared with them.

So, I did what I had to do—I adjusted. I took on a new identity, a little more mature, a little quieter. In the spirit of this new version of myself, I joined the Student Advisory Council so I could meet new people and make connections within my new community. Because I had to take out student loans to afford school, I also worked at a literacy center to help make ends meet. I threw myself into my studies, determined to be the best student I possibly could be.

Then, in the spring of 2000, I experienced a major confirmation of my faith during Spiritual Emphasis Week. Doug Oss was the speaker and one night he spoke about how we should seek God to find our calling. That night, I asked him to pray for me.

As we prayed, I saw an image in my mind. From where I stood, flat, hard ground extended as far as the eye could see before me. I started walking forward and as I did the ground behind me broke up with each step. When I turned to look back, I saw lush green grass, flowers, birds flitting in the clear blue sky, an idyllic landscape. But ahead of me, in the direction I was walking, was nothing but a wasteland.

I shared this scene with a couple of the church leaders and they thought I should consider church planting: starting a new church from scratch. Little did they know that was already on my mind. This experience was another confirmation that my calling was to start a new church.

But something was weighing on me.

I was still so lonely.

After the dates that went nowhere during my time as a youth pastor, not to mention the disastrous attempt to find some release by chatting online, I was really feeling the fact that I was single, and I felt it was time to find a girl and get married. People would joke around me that Bible College should actually be called "Bridal College," because everyone seemed to pair off and get married to their fellow students while attending.

But there I was, an eligible bachelor, ready to meet someone, but still chronically single.

Until I wasn't.

One of my duties at the Student Advisory Council was walking new students around for orientation. I would bring them around campus, point out the different buildings and points of interest, answer any questions they might have, that sort of thing. On one particular day, a group of girls showed up for the orientation walk, and among them was a shy, quiet girl named Jula.

She was with a bunch of friends, and when Jula was out of earshot, I asked them if she was single. They said she was. Then they told me they were all putting together this murder mystery dinner at their house, one of these gatherings where everyone dresses up as a different character, and they invited me to it.

So I went. I was one of four guys dressed up in costume at this dinner and she was there, so quiet and reserved—this mystery person at a mystery dinner. We all went bowling in our costumes afterwards and as the night was coming to a close, I asked her if she'd like to go on a date. She was so shy. She lowered her eyes and smiled. Then she said yes and gave me her phone number.

Turns out she hadn't dated before. She hadn't even kissed a guy. I wanted to be respectful and go slow, so before we went on our first one-on-one date, we went out on a group date to see a play. That's when we held hands for the first time, in the theater during the play. After that, we started going out, just the two of us. She didn't talk much, which was tough because I'm a talker. But she liked to listen to *me* talk. I shared some of my life story with her and I told her about some of the things I'd done in the ministry. She was always really impressed with what I'd done and she would look at me and say, "John, you're so wise."

Even though it felt really good to be listened to and she was such a sweet person, she was so painfully quiet that I was on the verge of breaking up with her.

But here's the thing: my father approved of her. My father, who was difficult to please, accepted her.

When I told him about how quiet she was and that I wasn't sure it was working out, he said, "Well, how have things gone dating sociable girls?" I knew what he meant—I hadn't had much luck dating any girls since breaking up with Laurie. So maybe a quiet girl would be the right fit for me. Really, the message from my father was that if she was quiet and likable, she would make a good minister's wife. And at this point I was focused on finding a wife that would be a good fit for the ministry and a good partner. In that regard, she was a perfect match.

So I took the plunge. I asked her to marry me.

I wanted the proposal to be a surprise, so I decided to propose on my twenty-seventh birthday in April 2001. I put together an elaborate plan with some friends to surprise her during my birthday dinner, where I had made reservations at a fancy Italian restaurant. I wanted to record the surprise, so my friends and I hid a video camera in the wine rack next to the table and a microphone in the flower centerpiece. The idea was that after I proposed, we would go back to her duplex where some of our closest friends would be waiting and we would all watch the video.

My friends were already at the restaurant before Jula and I arrived, ready to spring into action to make sure the surprise went according to plan. After we ate, I excused myself to use the restroom. As soon as I left, one of my friends started recording. Next, the manager of the restaurant came in on cue and gave Jula a bouquet of roses. She smiled and gave him a look like, "What's going on here?" Then the waitress came in with a cheesecake. We'd placed the diamond ring on top, and when Jula saw it her eyes grew big and she stared at it and shook her head and repeated, "Oh, my, my, my..."

And that's when I came in and got down on one knee.

"Jula," I said, "will you marry me?"

She was smiling with wide-eyed surprise and kept repeating, "My, my, my..." And then, "Yes!"

I put the ring on her finger and she looked at it and kept smiling and giggled sweetly.

We went back to her duplex after, where about fifteen or so of our closest friends were waiting for the party. I played the video of the proposal and everyone thought it was great; the recording had captured the moment perfectly.

Soon after we got engaged, my time at seminary school was coming to an end. I had my mind firmly set on starting my own church by now, and in May I went up to Kansas City with a friend to go to the International House of Prayer to get some guidance as to where I should establish it. This place was huge. There was one big dedicated prayer room with probably about two hundred people packed in there. Sometimes bands would be playing on the large stage up front and other times music played over the sound system. You couldn't talk to anyone in the main prayer room. It was just meant for around-the-clock prayer, nothing else.

In the back, on one of the side walls, there was a large map of the United States that covered the entire wall. People would stick tacks in it, marking places where they were praying for someone or some cause. I closed my eyes and prayed and walked back and forth in front of the map. Then I put my finger out and decided that wherever it landed was where I would go to start my church. I stopped pacing and planted my finger on the map.

I opened my eyes.

My finger landed smack-dab on Denver.

There was no question. A month later, I moved there. The idea was that Jula would come down once I'd raised enough money and was ready to start my church. Just before I left, I graduated from seminary school and my parents came to the ceremony. They hadn't come to my college graduation, which had really hurt, but they came this time since I was now following in my father's footsteps. Now I was going out to Denver to start my own ministry. It seemed like I was finally doing everything right.

But it wasn't meant to be. Five months later, I was right back in Springfield. Try as I might—and boy, I tried—I wasn't able to raise enough money. All my friends from seminary were asking what happened, why I'd come back. I just told them I'd put my plans on hold, but really, I was just afraid to tell them that I'd failed.

In November 2001, at Jula's church in North Carolina in the town where she grew up, Jula and I got married. My father presided over the ceremony. I'd only known Jula for eleven months at the time we got married. For five of those I had been in Denver. That's to say, we both had a lot to learn about each other.

Since things hadn't worked out in Denver, Jula and I decided to stay in Springfield, settle down a bit, and build our relationship. I ended up getting a job as a psychiatric technician at Lakeland Regional Hospital, what used to be, a behavioral health center for children and teenagers where I led groups mostly for adolescent girls. These girls were dealing with some really tough issues: alcohol and drug addiction, physical and sexual abuse, self-harming and cutting, you name it. Up until this point, I thought I'd been a good listener, but it wasn't until I started working with these girls that I truly started listening to what was going on inside.

One night, a fifteen-year-old girl I'd been working with looked up at me and said, "I wish you were my dad." Just like that. Out of the blue.

What do you say to that? At first, I was speechless. I just sat there for a moment and let the words set in. These kids were so vulnerable. They just needed to be accepted.

"Do you know what a diamond is?" I said.

"Of course I do," she said.

"I mean, do you know what a diamond is before it becomes a diamond?"

She shrugged like, "got me."

"Well, it starts off as a lump of coal. It's under the earth and it's getting squeezed down there and it's really hot, and after millions of years of heat and pressure, it emerges as a diamond."

She said she didn't know that's how diamonds were made.

"You know what you are? You're a diamond in the rough right now," I said. "You might feel dirty and dark and all that stuff, but just remember how that piece of coal started out. Eventually it will become a beautiful diamond that everyone will want."

I could tell that meant a lot to her. I'd never experienced anything like this before, this connection, this need for connection. These kids just wanted people to want them. I knew that feeling of wanting to be wanted, of just wanting someone to acknowledge you exist and that you matter, that you're cared about. I could relate to that. Like when I first met Jula and she listened to my stories and looked at me and said, "You're so wise." I had a deep need for that acknowledgment. I understood these girls because they taught me to listen not only to them, but to myself. I heard their souls, not just their words, because I could hear my soul too. And that's exactly what they wanted me to hear.

One day, another girl, Ashley, was taking a shower. At a certain point it seemed like it was taking a lot longer than usual. I asked a female colleague if she could go check on her. She went and immediately called me over and when I came into the room I found Ashley on the floor and there was blood all down her arm. She was cutting herself. I called a code 44—the highest emergency code—and within a matter of seconds fifteen to twenty staff showed up.

Meanwhile, I was by Ashley's side and I started feeling really strongly that I needed to tell her something, but it was something you're never supposed to say to a patient. There were a lot of reasons why you weren't supposed to tell a patient, "God loves you." But that's exactly what I said to her. Because I knew her. I'd talked to her and listened to her for weeks. And whether it was right or not, that's what I said, because I knew it was right for her.

The moment I said it, she dropped the metal object in her hand and started to cry.

"Why am I like this?" she said between sobs. "Why?"

I just said, "I don't know," and stayed by her side.

And that was the truth. I didn't know. I didn't have an answer. I wasn't going to make stuff up. I'd worked with her too long to insult her intelligence and start making stuff up now. Everyone who had responded to the code left, and a nurse and I took Ashley to the timeout room. She was transferred for observations for three days, and when she came back, she was a lot better.

Working at the hospital had a huge impact on me and I decided I wanted to get my master's in counseling. I figured it would be good to have a second degree to bolster my income, which would help fund my church. Even though it was really hard leaving a job that had been so transformative in my life, I knew I couldn't stay there forever. I had to move on and keep building my life.

In May 2003, we moved to the Newport News area of Virginia, where I enrolled at Regent University and Jula went in for her nursing degree. Still, the primary reason we moved down there was for me to start my own church at some point. We both got our degrees in 2005 and I still wasn't sure what the next step was, how I was going to proceed. The answer turned out to be pure serendipity.

During the time we were in Newport News, I had been golfing with some pastors from local churches. One day I was out with them and one of the pastors, Jim, said he knew a pastor of a local Assembly of God church who needed a children's pastor. I'm thinking, it's been great working with kids, but I'm not sure I want to be a children's pastor again. But Jim didn't waste any time. He got on the phone right there on the fairway and called the lead pastor up and handed me the phone.

I went in the next day to the Warwick Assembly of God for an interview and I got the job within a few weeks. They even hired me at a higher salary because of my two master's degrees. It was more money than I ever dreamed of making. I loved the job, the kids, the church. We even bought our first house, which was a big deal because I was really relying on this job now. Things looked like they were finally turning around.

One of the highlights of working at Warwick Assembly of God was living forty feet up in the air on a scissor lift for 168 hours—seven days straight. I had a small tent with an air mattress up there. I had a Porta-Potty. I had my laptop with Wi-Fi to connect with people. I had a bucket with a rope. I would lower the rope down to collect donations, and to collect my daily meals. Then I would pull it up and go from there. I had big banners on both sides of the scissor lift so that people could see that I was raising awareness and money for two charities: Project Rescue, which rescues girls out of sexual slavery, and Celebrate Recovery, a faith-based recovery program. In total, I raised $25,000 during those seven days.

Unfortunately, not too long after I landed the job, the lead pastor resigned. This was never a good thing because it's anyone's guess who's going to take that person's place. And sure enough, the minute the new pastor walked through the door, it was clear we weren't a good match. I left that job soon after.

Once again, my future was an open book.

CHAPTER 6

I Finally Hit My Stride

Not too long after leaving Warwick Assembly of God, an opportunity landed in my lap. A friend who was doing some fundraising in the area called and said he'd been talking to a pastor in Olympia, Washington, who was looking for a children's specialist for his church. I said I'd be happy to speak with him. Soon after, the lead pastor, named Dale, from Evergreen Christian Community called me. After we spoke, he came to visit us in Virginia and then flew me and Jula to Olympia for a five-day visit.

At one point when I was down there, I was talking with Dale about the potential job.

"So, John," he said, "what is it that really interests you in the position?"

"I'm not looking for a position," I replied.

He cocked his head and gave me a quizzical look.

Then I said, "You see, I already had a position in Virginia. So, I'm not looking for another position... I'm looking for a *purpose*."

Now a broad smile formed across his face.

"I'm really happy to hear that," he said, "because that's exactly the kind of person we want working with our kids. Someone who doesn't think of it just as a position... but a purpose, as you say."

Dale didn't want to hire just anyone. He wanted to hire someone who could grow the leadership team of the children's program, someone who had the vision to inspire children and leaders alike. In that moment, I was listening to myself and saying what I meant, just like those girls from Lakeland Regional taught me. That got me the job.

It was a big move and we had a lot to juggle. Since 2005, Jula's mother and her second husband had been living with us in Virginia. They didn't have to live with us; they weren't dependent or anything. But we loved Jula's mother and wanted her to be with us, so when we moved to Washington, they naturally came along. When Jula's mother asked if I could help her find a job in Olympia, I told Dale that my in-laws were coming with us and asked him about what kind of jobs were in the area that would be appropriate for them. Immediately he said he would hire them. And he did. He hired them to do custodial work around the church. This was a great sign of things to come in our working relationship.

In March 2007, with our Virginia home rented out, Jula and I hit the road for Olympia along with my in-laws and our two Alaskan malamutes.

Olympia was a totally different place from what I'd known on the East Coast: more relaxed, social justice–oriented, and environmentally conscious—all of which combined to make for a very unique culture. I had only known the stuffiness of the East Coast all my life, so it was a breath of fresh air. There was some culture shock, but it was a pleasant kind of culture shock. I instantly fell in love with the place.

Soon after I started at Evergreen, Dale pulled me into his office.

"Hey John, how are things going so far?" he asked from behind his desk.

"Fine," I said. "Still getting adjusted, but things are going good."

I was a little nervous. I had only been on the job for a couple of months or so. Had something gone wrong already?

"Perfect, that's great to hear," he said. "Listen, I was wondering—what's your character?"

I knew immediately what he meant. In the ministry, it's common for a youth minister to have a character—a playful persona the minister uses to entertain and educate the kids. Think Mickey Mouse or Goofy at Disney World. A costume. A funny voice. A range of quirky characteristics and sayings.

The only problem? I didn't have one.

But after just two months on the job, I'm not going to sit there and shrug and say to the lead pastor, nope, sorry, never had a character, haven't done that. So what do I do?

It came to me on the spot. Back in college, my best friend had a nickname for me. He called me Butter because of how he observed me interacting and networking with people—as in, "Smooth as Butter." When a speaker would come to campus, I would always go right up to that person afterwards and just start talking and networking. Yup, smooth as butter, all right.

Sitting there in that office with Dale expectantly waiting for the great character I didn't have, I blurted out: *"Butter!"*

"Butter?" he said. He scrunched up his eyes and shook his head. "What kind of character is that?"

"He's a rapper."

Sure. Why not?

"Okay," said Dale. "Why is his name Butter?"

"Cuz he's smooth and he's spreading the news," I said off the top of my head.

And that did it. Dale just burst out laughing. He loved it. That became Butter's tagline.

And that's more or less how my tenure at Evergreen began—spontaneously. As I did throughout my time there, I had to think on my toes, be creative, take chances.

In that moment, Butter was born. I threw together the costume: a silver velvet tuxedo blazer and pants, six-inch silver high-top shoes from the 70s disco era, and a great big frizzy black wig. I even went so far as to have a dentist make a mold of my top row of teeth so I could make fake silver teeth that I would snap on when I'd transform into Butter. Throw in some aviator sunglasses, gold and silver chains, and some oversized rings, and the transformation was complete. I looked like some twisted version of the Mad Hatter. Minus the hat.

Butter was a hit. The kids loved him. He would often appear at the end of Sunday meetings to wrap up the lesson and sometimes we'd make music videos with Butter and the kids rapping. I wanted to keep Butter special for the kids, so I only brought him out occasionally. It worked. I'd keep Butter's appearances a secret, and when he'd come out, the kids would go crazy because they hadn't seen him for a while and weren't expecting him.

Once, we had a fundraising competition between the boys and the girls. The girls won and they got to have a sleepover in one of the main event rooms at the church. I told the mothers who were chaperoning the event that at midnight we would play Butter's intro song (everyone knew Butter's song by now) and I'd come out as Butter and surprise everyone. When we played the music and I came out, you would have thought Zac

Efron had just strutted onto the stage. They went absolutely crazy.

When I was done with my bit, I said, "Butter's on roll! Butter's got to go!"

And that's when the girls rushed the stage. They started pulling at my costume. I couldn't get off stage.

"Um, can I get some moms to give Butter a hand, Butter can barely stand!"

That's when the moms came onstage and helped peel away the girls, but I could tell they let it drag out, they were enjoying it so much.

Sure, it was a lot of fun, but it took a ton of work to make Butter and the entire children's program come together. Evergreen was much bigger than Warwick. Warwick was about 250 parishioners large. Evergreen was more than four times as big, with 1,100 parishioners, and after the four years I was there, it grew to 1,700.

My leadership responsibilities grew in kind. As the children's specialist, I oversaw all kid's programs from birth through fifth grade, covering three Sunday church services and a growing roster of activities. But to support these activities and to grow the church, my leadership responsibilities branched out significantly into outreach, fundraising, and staff and volunteer development.

In 2008, I decided I would do a fundraising event called "Up in the Air". This meant that I would be lifted up in the air on a scissor lift for a week, not allowed to come down, with a tent, a Porta-Potty, and the intention of reaching a monetary goal for an exceptional cause. I thought it would work as a great fundraiser for the church. There was a new shopping center in town, and I thought it would be the perfect spot. If approximately 20,000 cars went through and donated $1, that would be $20,000 each day. So, we gave it a go. Unfortunately, it didn't go as planned. We made some money, but not nearly the $20,000 a day that I had dreamed. After the event, I felt like God was telling me, "Yes, John. That would've been amazing. You see 20,000 people hopefully giving a dollar. I see millions of people that won't take a moment just to say thank you for the day." This was enlightening to me. I was certainly thankful for all the money raised for a good cause, but now I had a new perspective. I would use this strategy a few more times throughout my life's ministry.

Later that year, the church sent me on a trip to Thailand and China. Helping others and driving a mission has always been very important to me, so I proposed that we look for a specific project that our kids and their families could support. I met with members of the local government in the Kunming region of southwest China where they were trying to find ways for the struggling small villages there to be more economically self-sustaining. They identified goat farming as a viable means for the villages to become more economically independent.

Back home, we got back "up-in-the-air" and we were able to raise $25,000. But it was the kids who helped spread awareness of the issue and really drove the fundraising efforts; it was the kids and their parents who raised all that money. Those funds went straight to those poor villages in China to help them start goat farming.

By now I had built a large, involved team of leaders and volunteers. It's tough getting people to stand up and volunteer to work in a children's department at a church. People have to sacrifice some evenings and especially weekends and work with kids. It's tough work, and not everyone's cut out for it, or they just want to relax on the weekends and have family time. But because of the vision and direction we were able to create, we were able to amass a large team of volunteers to really help drive the increased number of kids and activities at the church.

That doesn't just happen by itself. A lot of pastors will just have a need and they'll enlist people to go in and fill that need, whether or not the people are skilled or passionate about the work. When I was younger, the only people I would see up on stage at church was the pastor—in my case, my father—or evangelists and missionaries brought in as guests. I never saw people like me or my friends or people from around town. I never saw *everybody else*.

That's not how I rolled. I was always looking to see how I could get people truly involved in a project, how I could network with people and pair them with the right projects and get them spiritually or emotionally invested. Not just plop them in a hole that needs to be filled. To me, God doesn't just call people to be ministers, evangelists, and missionaries. God calls people to do everything: to be a painter, a doctor, a mechanic. Everything. It doesn't matter what it is. All of these people are just as valuable and just as capable of making meaningful contributions to the world and to the church.

At Evergreen, if someone had an interest, I found a place for them where they could make a contribution.

My first few months there, I was thinking about how I could get more parent volunteers involved in the ministry. Then, I had an idea gifted to me. That Sunday, within the video announcements of all the church happenings, I added my own announcement.

The video showed me sitting at Olive Garden and sharing that I love the kids, but I really miss talking with all of the parents. There's some great things happening in their kids' lives and I want them to hear all about it. I then went on to explain that out in the lobby, there were tables with sign up sheets for the next four months. Anyone could sign up for one night to go out to eat with me, and I'd pay for it.

After the first Sunday, the calendar was practically filled up. I was busy for the next four months getting to know the parents of ECC and getting them into places that they could help serve. For example, there was a father that worked with computers. He asked, "I'm not sure what I can do to help." I told him that we needed someone to run our children's check in and out system in the mornings. He was completely confident that he could do that. There was another woman who wanted to know how to volunteer with a nonprofit organization. I told her not to worry and I would show her how. It was really neat for me to meet with the faces of our church community and get to know who the people are as well as get them involved.

It wasn't long before I had enough volunteers to start setting up kid's clubs. They weren't doing anything of the sort when I first got there. At the Wednesday night kid's ministry, they would just throw on a video and have the kids sit there and watch. I completely changed that around. We got a craft club and drama club going. We got a computer and car club going. The message to the kids was: you can serve God and do anything. Not just become a pastor. Not just become a missionary. You can be an artist, an actor, a computer scientist, a car mechanic.

One day while in the middle of brainstorming groups for our kids in the office at Evergreen Christian Community, one of the pastors stopped in and introduced me to a man named Robert. Turns out, he was actually the owner and teacher of the Mixed Martial Arts studio right next to the church's property. So, we walked over to Robert's gym and had a look. He had a space to practice Martial Arts, but also had a side set up for CrossFit. He invited me to come and join one of his classes sometime.

The next week, I took him right up on his offer and started Brazilian Jiu Jitsu and CrossFit. This was my first experience with either sport, but I can assure you that Brazilian Jiu Jitsu is no joke. I mean those guys were good. Each time we would roll on the mats, I would end up tapping out. It was humbling, but inspiring as well. I lost forty pounds between the two classes in six months. Robert was so helpful, kind, and authentic, so I wondered if he would be willing to help the kids at church.

One day, I just asked him if he would be comfortable donating some of his time to teaching ten to fifteen kids Brazilian Jiu Jitsu once a week on Wednesday nights for about forty-five minutes at his gym. He quickly responded with, "Absolutely, man! Let's do it!" Before long, we had the group set up and were taking about twelve kids over to his gym to begin learning jiu jitsu. The kids loved it, their parents loved it, Robert loved it, and I loved it. That's how I got him involved. He wasn't part of the team before; now he was.

I really started to hone in on this idea of a style of leadership centered around building relationships with people and decided I wanted to do more to become the most effective leader possible for those I served. I decided to enroll in the Missional Leadership doctoral program at the Assemblies of God Theological Seminary. I studied remotely, but three times a year I would fly to Springfield to attend class on campus.

Meanwhile, of course, life went on. In 2008, the financial crisis rocked the world. Back in Virginia, the house we still owned and were renting out went under water: we owed more than the house was worth. We tried to get a short sale, but when that didn't work out, we walked away and ended up filing for Chapter 11 bankruptcy, which gave us five years to pay off our obligation. So much for that. Pretty much overnight, a good financial investment turned into a huge financial liability.

At the same time, after about seven or eight years, my marriage with Jula was beginning to fray. Communication was breaking down and things had grown downright cold between the sheets. While I was working at the church, she was working as a nurse. I would come home from a full day of work at the church, and she would come home from twelve-hour shifts at the hospital. Our lives felt like they were worlds apart. When we'd check in at night, I thought I was doing a good job keeping her up-to-date with everything going on at the church, but she started to become more and more upset.

"Why don't you tell me anything?" she would say.

I would throw my hands in the air. "I do tell you. I tell you all the time."

Then she began to ask why I was doing things a certain way at church functions. I wasn't sure how to explain what I was doing at my job. One of the reasons I married her was because she was such a good listener, but I didn't feel like she was listening to me anymore. It felt like she was just questioning and challenging me, and I had enough to answer for as a pastor. She no longer said, "John, you're so wise." I never heard those words again. Instead, she kept working to understand me.

On top of that, we both wanted children, but because of these difficulties nothing was happening in that department. People at church started asking about when we were planning on having children. A children's pastor is expected to have children, so those kinds of questions were not unusual. And of course, I wanted kids, and so did Jula. But we didn't know what to do. We came up with a bunch of reasons: we were waiting for the right time; we were "working" on it; we were delaying until I was done with my studies.

None of it was true. They were all lies. I found myself in this very difficult place: here I was a pastor of a church and it's like I was living in a glass house. As a pastor, I was frequently counseling people on their own intimacy issues and I couldn't even be honest about my own. I couldn't tell people the truth. I was stuck living a lie, this version of what people expected me to be: a happy married man with plans for a family on the way. But I wasn't happy, and neither was Jula. And we didn't have plans for a family on the way. I considered relationship-building one of my greatest strengths, but in the most sacred relationship of all—marriage—I was a fraud.

During this time, I'm grateful I had a great group of friends to blow off steam with. It became a tradition to watch the UFC fights with the guys at my place. It was a pretty big deal. There were about a dozen of us. We'd pile a table full of sandwiches and snacks and load up the cooler with drinks and hunker down for the fight. All night long we would laugh, joke, tease each other, tell stories, and just be downright rowdy. I really miss that joyful feeling of hanging out with the boys.

It was during this time of struggles with my wife that I experienced a darkness, an unshakable sense of gloom and inevitability. I didn't know what it was at the time. I didn't know what I know now—that it had been there all along, since childhood, building. I know now that it was depression. I suffered from it since I was much younger and would battle it throughout my adult life. At the time it was just this darkness, this clinging, cloying thing, this monkey on my back. All I could do was work through it. Work harder, do more, make more happen, meet more people, whatever the case—just do more.

Ultimately, I blamed myself when I couldn't get out of bed or had to call in sick to work. But for the most part, I was able to push through it. For now.

All the worries and questions about having children were resolved on September 28, 2010, when my son Jaxson was brought into the world. Jula and I resolved to move forward with conception of our first child through artificial insemination. I was overjoyed with the birth of my son and my career couldn't have been better at this point. But Jula and I were beginning to encounter difficulties, and so long as I was a pastor, there was no way out. We were keeping up appearances. That was never how I wanted to live my life.

CHAPTER 7

Finding My Purpose

At this point, I had a wife and a beautiful baby boy and a job that I loved in Olympia. We lived in a lovely home with my in-laws and our two malamutes. I had wide latitude to build the children's program in Olympia and was widely respected. Even if, in the larger picture, I still had lots of unresolved questions to work out in my personal and spiritual life, it seemed after years of constant stops and starts, things had finally hit their stride.

At Evergreen Christian Community, we had small groups. This was a time when people of similar interests, ages, or stages of life would meet during the week in between regular services. At this time, I was one of the leaders. As the children's minister, I naturally led a group full of parents with young children or who were a part of the children's ministry. We would meet every two weeks, every other Friday, at a church member's home who had enough room to hold everyone - parents and kids. During our get-togethers, we would often find a babysitter to come and watch the children downstairs so the parents and adults could have some intentional quality time together. It was always a great time.

Most people in Olympia are very skeptical and sometimes even cynical of any faith or church. However, with this mentality surrounding them, David and his wife Rhiannon began coming to our church anyway. When I met the two of them, even though they were already believers, they were unsure of the church scene. There was some hesitation to getting involved in different church activities and such on their end. Knowing this, I thought that our small group scene might be less overwhelming. So, I explained that it's normal people, just like them and I, who eat, hang out, and have discussions surrounding our faith. Eventually, I was able to convince them to come.

On the next small group meetup, David and Rhiannon came. I was so excited to see them there. We ate, laughed, and shared quality conversations as a whole group. As we wrapped things up, I walked them out to their car. I asked, "Well, did you guys enjoy our small group?"

"We actually enjoyed it very much," David and his wife agreed. "We'd like to come back next time as well."

"Great! That's awesome!" I exclaimed.

"In fact," David continued. "We had a code word to tell the other, just in case we didn't like it."

I said, "What?!"

"Yeah, we had a code word already planned out." David chuckled.

"What would happen if you used the code word?" I asked.

David explained, "Well, if either of us were uncomfortable with the small group situation at any point during the evening we could say, 'Muskrat'. As soon as we heard 'Muskrat', we knew it was time to just get up, get your coat, and leave." We all immediately began a marvelous belly laugh at the whole situation. I was so glad that neither David nor Rhiannon used the code word, 'Muskrat'. They continued their faith walk within our church and that story still brings a giggle to my soul.

After four years with Evergreen Christian Community, Dale, the lead pastor, decided to relocate to Fresno, California. When the new pastor came in to take his place, one by one the rest of the ten pastors who remained began to leave, including me. This run of luck had just run out.

And yet, sometimes change comes just when you're ready for it. Even before I started as a children's minister in Olympia, I knew I wanted to move on to something else. I had two master's degrees and was working on my doctorate; it just felt like the time had come. Now, with Dale's departure, I had an opportunity to make a transition to something more elevated. In the back of my mind, the vision of that desolate, rocky plain in front of me as I'm walking away from those blooming flowers and blue skies had stuck with me. I maintained a sense that I was destined for a higher calling—and that calling was to plant my own church. I knew it was still a few years off, but I needed to start turning in that direction.

I had been sending out my resume to other opportunities once Dale left and a few months later got a call from lead pastor Frank of Albany First Assembly in Albany, Oregon (now Hope Church). He asked me if I would be interested in an executive role. Albany First Assembly is one of the largest mission-driven Assemblies of God churches in the country. It is well known for its community-based work with an eye towards global change, what it calls *Across the Street and Around the World.* This was an incredible opportunity.

"Come on out and we'll show you around," he said once I told him I was interested. "We'd like your whole family to see the church... and you can do a formal interview with the board."

We went down and arrived at First Albany on a Sunday morning. The minute we got there, I almost turned right around and walked out. Right off the bat, I felt unwelcomed. There wasn't a friendly feeling to the place at all. Jaxson was six months old at the time, so when we arrived, we immediately needed to go to the nursery. An older man showed us to the nursery. When we got there, we handed Jaxson over to the woman in charge along with a clean diaper and a bottle ready to go with formula. We said that he was recently changed and might get hungry while they gave us a tour of the church. The woman just looked at me and shook her head.

"Oh, no," she said. "I'm sorry, we don't feed babies or change diapers."

Don't feed babies or change diapers? In a church nursery? I almost lost it! In Olympia, where we had 1,700 parishioners, I was in charge of the children's program, including the nursery. First Albany had around eight hundred parishioners at the time. Not quite as many as Olympia, but still a good-sized church, and they couldn't do something as basic as feed a baby and change its diaper? It was a no-brainer. You don't even think about it, you just do it.

The older man must have seen the look on my face, because I'm sure it was red hot. He stepped in and said, "We will take care of that. No problem at all."

I didn't know it at the time, but the man was a board member. He looked a little sheepish, like he knew this was an embarrassing shortcoming but was doing his best to make it right.

We went to the auditorium for service. *I don't want to be here*, I thought as we sat and waited for service to start. But what were we supposed to do, walk right out before service? For the most part the service turned out to be fine, as did the pastor's sermon. If only it wasn't for the music! They had an old-school choir singing songs that had gone out of date decades ago. Church choirs have come back in fashion these days, but at the time this was the kind of music you might find in a church in the 70s, not 2011. Compared to Olympia, with its fully outfitted symphony orchestras playing on holidays and its spiritual bands, this church was living in the Dark Ages.

That afternoon, I sat down with the church leadership for my final interview.

"So, how are you finding things so far?" asked the pastor Frank.

At first I had to bite my tongue; I felt like I'd been holding it in for ages. In this case, honesty was not only the best policy, it was the only policy.

"Well, do you want the unvarnished truth? Or do you just want me to make it sound good?" I asked.

Pastor Frank clasped his hands and gave a slight nod and grin. He seemed to know this was coming. "The unvarnished truth, please. We need to hear it."

I told them about my experience at the nursery.

"How do you expect to attract families to your church if you can't even tend to the most important thing in people's lives? Their children?"

They understood, though they didn't seem to be aware of the problem. I mentioned the music too and they acknowledged it was something they had been trying to improve. All in all, I told them my impressions: the good, the bad, and the ugly.

In the end, they were looking for someone to come in with a fresh pair of eyes to evaluate these kinds of things. After the interview, they offered me the job. I accepted because this is what I was basically born to do—to come in and turn a church around in the face of mounting challenges. To build relationships and build a community. I may not have loved my first visit, but this was just the kind of challenge I relished.

We packed up and moved again: me, Jula, Jaxson, my in-laws, and our two malamutes. My in-laws ended up staying in Albany for only nine months before they moved to Fresno where Dale, the former pastor in Olympia, lined them up with more custodial work, since there simply wasn't any work for Koreans in Albany at the time. It was mostly all white people up there.

In my role as Executive Pastor of Spiritual Life, I set out to do exactly what I said I would do, and basically did the job of two full-time pastors. I got off the ground running, directing Bible groups, counseling families, raising money (including more "up-in-the-air" fundraisers), and hosting events. I even brought in a black Christian comedian to perform. Mind you, this was nothing new or revolutionary, but for Albany it was like the dawning of a new era!

At one point a few months in, Pastor Frank said to me, "I have to say, you're doing a fine job. You really think outside the box, don't you?"

I thanked him and said that, yes, thinking outside the box was one of my greatest strengths.

Pastor Frank chuckled and said, "I want you to know what I'm about to tell you next is a compliment."

"Okay, what is it?"

"I highly doubt if you've ever done anything *inside* the box."

True enough.

One of my greatest lasting legacies at Albany, or at any church, was the massive Hispanic outreach program I started there. The way that program developed was all about thinking outside the box. Of all things, that program had its origins not in an email campaign or knocking on doors or going around to local businesses or big events—but in handing out hot dogs, potato chips, and soda.

This may take some explaining.

It all started with one of the missionary guests I had come down to work with the church. He was this crazy, wild-haired guy who looked like he might have just come in off the streets, but he was a dynamo of missionary work. He worked with communities in East St. Louis, one of the poorest areas in the country. I wanted him to come to Albany to shake things up a bit. Someone who did missionary work in East St. Louis surely could teach us a thing or two in Albany.

And he did indeed shake things up. One of the stories of his missionary work stuck with us about how he would drive to one of the worst parts of East St. Louis with a trailer and set up a little food cart and cook up some hot dogs and burgers. Then he would hand out free hot dogs, burgers, chips, and soda to anyone who wanted them. That's it. No preaching. No recruiting. He just handed out free food for those who needed it.

My guys at Albany loved the idea. "Why don't we do that here?" they asked.

We did it, of course. Once a month, we packed up a truck and went out into the community and cooked up hot dogs and hamburgers. We handed them out with soda and chips to around a hundred people for free. No preaching. No recruiting. We were servants of God, giving to the community where there was need.

About six months into this, we noticed some more and more Hispanics were coming. None of us knew Spanish, so we recruited Sonia, a woman from the church who spoke Spanish, to join us and help hand out food. She went out and started spreading the word about the free food to Hispanics in the community and they started asking her if she could teach them English.

"Pastor John," she said when she came back, "they're asking me if we can teach them English. What should I tell them?"

I'm sitting there thinking: *I don't have a clue how to do that!* But is that what I told her?

I looked at Sonia and said, "Tell them we can."

Sonia's eyes grew big and she looked bewildered. "But how?" she asked.

"I don't know," I said candidly, shrugging, "but I'll figure it out."

How many people would have just said, "Nope, I'm sorry, we don't do that?" And that would be that? But that's never been my way. As Pastor Frank pointed out, I've never done anything inside the box. I've always worked outside the box. Why would I fall back now?

In less than a week, I contacted a retired Assemblies of God missionary who ran a nonprofit group in another city that taught English as a second language out of a local church. I asked her if she could help us do a similar program in Albany and she agreed. We ended up recruiting twenty of our adults who wanted to volunteer for two Saturdays a month and trained and certified them on teaching English as a second language. Then we launched the program.

From giving out hot dogs, chips, and soda to connecting with the Hispanic community to partnering with a nonprofit teaching English as a second language, we were now teaching forty adults to speak English as volunteers took care of their children. Yup. I got that nursery turned around big time, too. The Hispanic program is still running today at Hope Church.

Another ministry I helped start in Albany, was called Celebrate Recovery. This was a faith-based twelve step program for people who have "hurts, habits, and hang-ups." The goal of this group was to provide support and strategies to help individuals move forward and get past some of their hurts, habits, and hang-ups. A gentleman named Barry took over the leadership role of this ministry. I only helped initially to get him on the ground and running. Once he was on his feet, he had that program rolling. There were often 70-80 individuals in attendance on Thursday nights. On those nights, there would be a full meal and then they would break out into individualized small groups and have their discussions

I couldn't help but sit back and reflect on my time so far. Here was a church that I felt like I wanted to walk away from the moment I first walked through the door. But instead, I was able to take everything I had learned over the years about relationship-building and build a stronger community there. I gave it my all.

I thought I might use another "Up in the Air" fundraiser in 2014 to which part of the proceeds would go towards Project Rescue. The idea made me reflect back on the people that attended Evergreen Christian Community who were so great to support this unique fundraiser. Like I did there, I challenged my current church members to donate or collect exactly $168. I decided on $168 since I would be up on the scissor lift for 168 hours and it would cover most of the trip. After the fundraiser was announced, a man named Nick approached me with his girlfriend and daughter. "You're not going to believe this," he said.

I looked at him a bit shocked. "Believe what?" I questioned.

"I looked in my wallet to see what I have to donate and I have exactly $168 in my wallet." He said, shocked and smiling. My eyes widened and I smiled. Indeed, what an encouragement this was.

"Up in the Air" was successful and in the summer of 2010, I traveled to India with five other individuals. The trip had two purposes, first to teach some children's leadership seminars at Southern Asia Bible College. Second, to see firsthand the operations of Project Rescue, the organization that saves women from sex slavery.

We were guided by a Project Rescue team member through downtown to the Red Lights District. Our guide informed us that within this eight block area, there were thousands of enslaved girls. There I was halfway across the world, standing in what looks like a dirty alleyway between two buildings. There, up on the second floor is a caged young girl with a hopeless face. It was an emotional roller coaster at that moment. I felt anger. I felt sadness. I felt discouraged to try and change such a huge industry. I was overcome with the urge to do something about it. How could I save all of them? The vastness of this issue is a dark and endless hole. But, what if I could change one girl's life. Then, I can save another girl's life. Then another, just going at it one at a time. It was worth a try. I had to try. I just had to.

After our walk down the Red Light District, we went back to a "Home of Hope," one of the places that houses girls who have been rescued. I noticed two young girls that were so thrilled to see us. They were willing to share their stories of being enslaved and then rescued. Soon, many of the other girls began to share their stories too. It was wonderful to hear stories of such redemption and hope. It was heartbreaking to see how girls are used and abused in India. However, I am thankful for ministries like Project Rescue that are there to make a difference as best they can. It was a life-changing trip that has made me a lifelong advocate of this amazing humanitarian effort.

Because of this experience, I came home determined to join them in their humanitarian efforts. Then, my thoughts journeyed back to Olympia and Phil. Phil was one of the pastors that I had worked with. He had traveled to New York, ran a marathon, and came back to our pastors meeting and shared what the experience had taught him. As the competitive personality that I am, I looked him up and down. Now, mind you Phil was physically your 'average joe'. He did a great job, but he wasn't exactly bleeding athleticism. I decided that if Phil completed a marathon then I could definitely run one - but I added a twist.

I decided I would use my marathon training as a way to fundraise to help stop the sex trafficking and sex slavery in India. I trained for months and finally ran in the San Diego Rock 'n' Roll Marathon in 2012 to raise $25,000 in sponsorship funds for Project Rescue. My mind wandered back to the stories of those girls who had been rescued. I hoped that my church's contribution would help just one girl break away and find freedom. I got an extra reward: losing fifty-five of my then 270 pounds! I ended up using this idea again to run the same marathon again in 2013 and then did two triathlons in 2014.

My career was taking off. Everything should have been great. But the darkness I had started experiencing in Olympia was still there. The "monkey on my back," as I called it. It wasn't there constantly, but enough that several times I had to call in sick to work. Even with all of the running, biking, and swimming I was doing to train for marathons, I was still fighting depression.

During these times, I didn't want to see anyone, but I still didn't know why. I didn't know it was depression. I didn't know it wasn't my fault when it descended upon me.

One day I went to bed and didn't get out till eighteen days later. I didn't go to church. I didn't show up for work. I didn't go out to get groceries. Nothing. I told everyone that I had come down with bacterial pneumonia. But that was just another cover to keep up appearances.

I had no idea what was happening, why I was feeling this way. I picked apart all the little things I thought I'd done wrong. A missed email. An event that didn't go quite as I'd hoped. I thought I could have done more to help. I blamed myself. All these little perceived failures just added up and in some way, I felt I was a failure, too.

I managed to push through it and on May 21, 2012, Jula and I had our second child—our son Jentzen. This was the second-best day of my life. The first, of course, being the day my first son was born.

So here I was: I had a wife and two beautiful children and a job that was booming. But my mind was still turning back to those flowers and blue skies, and away from that flat, rocky wasteland in my dream.

This is when the thought of church planting really started taking root. I had worked for many failing churches and butted heads with many strict, conservative pastors, so I had developed a clear vision for what I wanted to do differently. It was the subject of my doctoral thesis, and I wanted to bring it to life. I pictured a church based on relationships. I wanted it to be less conservative and more about people going out to serve people in the community and less about people coming to the church. I just didn't know when I was going to do it and where it was going to be.

Then I got my answer. Quite literally, it was given to me.

It happened in August 2013 on a visit to see leading Assembly of God Pastor Choco de Jesus speak at the Assembly of God General Council meeting, something of a conference for pastors held once every two years in Orlando. Choco de Jesus is one of the foremost preachers in the world, a leader who has appeared on the cover of *Time* magazine.

He was speaking in an auditorium about twelve thousand large and I was about twenty-five rows back. When he was done speaking, there were hundreds of people packed up to the stage to pray with him. Most people from where I was standing probably would have just said, "Well, next time maybe I'll get to pray with Choco."

But suddenly I felt like God was telling me to go pray with Choco. I turned to the group I was with and told them this and headed for the stage. I pushed through the massive crowd and managed to squeeze my way to the front. I waited; there was no guarantee he would come my way, but then he turned and before I knew it, he was towering over me. He put his right hand on my head and held my left hand, which I had raised into the air.

It hit me when Choco placed his hand on my head. A vision. A true vision. At that moment, I heard exactly what I had to do. God said, "Yes, John, you will plant a church. It will be two years from now in San Diego."

I heard God's message in my heart and started to cry.

I knew right there and then that when I returned to Albany, I would tell Pastor Frank my plans and begin transitioning out of my role there and into the next chapter of my life in San Diego. When I returned and told him about my life-changing prayer experience with Choco, I was relieved to find that Pastor

Frank was happy for me and supportive. We made a plan that I would move to San Diego in August of 2015. But we agreed that we wouldn't announce the transition until just before the move about a year later.

Over the next few months I made several trips to San Diego to scout out neighborhoods where I might plant my church. Even though I was excited, second thoughts were beginning to bubble up. I started thinking the whole idea was impossible, and it all came down to money. Would I be able to raise enough money to start my own church? How? No number of "up-in-the-air" fundraisers would be enough to raise the kind of money I would need. San Diego wasn't exactly cheap. And I had a family to raise. It wasn't like there would be a church waiting for me out there with a built-in community and support. I was planting my own church. I had to grow it myself. But how?

Then, as I was on my way to Starbucks on Valentine's Day in 2014, I looked over and saw a guy driving next to me. He had a scripture verse tattooed on his arm: *Isaiah 41:10*. The moment I pulled into Starbucks and parked, I took out my phone and looked up the verse.

So do not fear, for I am with you;
do not be dismayed, for I am your God.
I will strengthen you and help you;
I will uphold you with my righteous right hand.

When I read these words, I had the overwhelming feeling that God was speaking to me. It was like Choco was placing his hand on my head again. He would handle the money issue. I didn't need to worry. That was what I needed to know. I was ready.

In May 2014, the church announced my planned departure to the community. Everyone was excited for me and supportive of my decision. By this time, I had made a plan with Pastor Frank that I would stay on through July 2015, a little over a year from now, when I would be participating in my first Ironman in Coeur d'Alene, Idaho. I had started training more than a year in advance. This included two triathlons to prepare for Ironman's grueling 2.4-mile swim, 112-mile bike ride, and 26.2-mile run.

But in November, during a trip to Pennsylvania to raise money and attend the Assemblies of God Church Planting Boot Camp to prepare for my move to San Diego, Pastor Frank called and said he wanted to meet with me when I get back. There was something about the way he sounded that gave me a bad feeling.

When I returned and met with Pastor Frank, he said, "I bet you're getting excited about the San Diego church plant, John."

This seemed like a way to soften whatever he was going to say next. I responded that I was excited and that I had a lot of work to do between now and then.

Then he laid it on me.

"John, you need to know that you're not in the 2015 budget."

"What do you mean?" I asked, barely able to believe what he was saying.

"Well... I mean your salary isn't budgeted for 2015."

"But we had an understanding, Frank. You committed to keeping me on through Ironman."

He looked at me square in the eyes and said, "Maybe we can give you a few months through March. How about that? Let me look into it."

A few months through March didn't make any sense in terms of my preparations and planning. No matter which way I cut it, Pastor Frank's decision to cut me out of the budget left me feeling like I was getting mugged and sideswiped. This change of course would mess up my entire exit strategy.

But what was I supposed to do? He was the lead pastor. He'd clearly made up his mind. It's not like arguing with him was going to make a difference. I decided to make the best of it and hoped that this was just a bump in the road as I turned away from that flat, rocky plain in my dream towards those blue skies and green meadows that would be my church in San Diego.

CHAPTER 8

Losing the Will to Live

We left for San Diego on April 1, 2015. In retrospect, it seems cruelly ironic, even a bad omen, that we moved on April Fool's Day. But at the time, it didn't even register. I was laser-focused on the road ahead, both literally and figuratively. It had been fourteen years exactly since my dream of turning away from the wasteland of indecision towards the brighter future of planting my own church, and this was finally the moment. My plan may have been nearly upended in Oregon, but I was on my way and I was determined. Once again, I moved my family to another city. Only this time, I was convinced that it would be different. This time, we were settling down in the beautiful city of San Diego where God had told me I was destined to plant my own church.

Moving to San Diego was both awesome and awful, beautiful and brutal, courageous and crushing. I loved San Diego, the people, the spirit of the city, and I was excited to get working. But I was almost completely on my own with zero guarantee of success. There's no blueprint for church planting. You can attend all the boot camps in the world and it still comes down to a whole lot of chance. The process is constantly fluid, shifting and changing beneath your feet based on local dynamics and a whole host of unknowns. Ultimately, because of this, there's a high rate of failure.

But I had in place what I thought was a strong strategy. It was twofold: it consisted of an aggressive campaign of relationship-building backed by fundraising through the church. Even if Pastor Frank had essentially cut me loose, I was still affiliated with the Assemblies of God church in Oregon. Before I left for San Diego, I had set up an agreement with the church whereby they would manage the funds I raised. This took some pressure off the business end of things and it was one less thing I had to worry about. I also continued to raise funds through the Assemblies of God network of churches to support my church-planting efforts on the ground in San Diego.

My primary goal with respect to relationship-building was to meet twenty-five new people each week. It was part of what's called the "funnel strategy," in church-planting lingo. The idea is to meet a certain number of people each week and keep building your roster of relationships, while "funneling" all of these contacts through various stages of development. By the end of two months, meeting twenty-five people a week, I should conceivably connect with two hundred people. As I move through the process, some contacts will drop off and some will remain, and those who remain could constitute my future flock.

Building relationships starts off relatively easy, but as you go into months two and three, it gets more and more difficult as it becomes harder to meet the same number of people each week. Not only are the people harder to find, but the work of investing in every relationship you build takes its toll. If you're serious about truly connecting with people as people, and not just as a means to an end, no one person is any less important than the next. This can become emotionally draining.

Not only did I set myself the mandate to meet twenty-five people a week, but I also had to keep on top of fundraising to support relationship-building events and my future church. Events I hosted included a Mother's Day brunch in 2015 for which I brought runner-up *Master Chef* contestant Natasha Crnjac as a celebrity chef to cook the meal. Another event I organized was a Father's Day block party. To drum up interest, I went out with my son Jaxson and put seven hundred door-hangers with information about the church and block party on the doors of people in the community. I had rented out a park in the neighborhood and we strung up balloons and had face painting, games, and inflatables, and served hamburgers and hot dogs.

The whole idea was to just make it a fun event for the community, not some preachy information session about the church. I wanted people who came to understand that this was about building a community, not sitting around and listening to someone talk about the church. Around thirty-five people ended up coming. Not an overwhelming turnout, to be sure. But for me, it wasn't about the numbers. I didn't have a number for success. It was about connecting with whoever came and building those specific relationships. Maybe the connection would lead to the church, and maybe it wouldn't. Maybe a connection was meant for something else; I was okay with that. That's a major part of my philosophy of relationship-building. It's not about the church, it's about the people.

When the Father's Day event was over, I followed up with the attendees to see if they wanted to come to a gathering at my house. Some people came, some didn't. That's the "funnel" strategy in action. You start by meeting large numbers of people, knowing a bunch aren't going to commit to coming to events, but with each event, the ones that do come and keep coming might just become a church member in time.

In time. That was the thorn in my side. Time.

While I was having some success at events and meeting new people, my fundraising goals were slipping away. Without funding, I was dead in the water. I had known that money would be the determining factor in the success of my church planting. It was the sole reason I had doubted moving forward, until I saw the tattoo on that man's arm—*Isaiah 41:10*:

So do not fear, for I am with you... I will uphold you with my righteous right hand...

He had me covered. I need not worry. He would provide.

But I was beginning to worry. I was beginning to fear. The money was slipping away.

I had raised about $150,000 prior to the move, but some of that had already been spent before the day of the move to develop promotional materials, such as a professional fundraising video I could send to people, and to create a website. There was already quite a bit of money out the door on day one and I ended up having to raise at least $8,000 a month to support the events I was hosting.

For the first month or so, $8,000 may be a doable amount to raise, but it only gets harder to maintain that level of fundraising as time goes on. But soon I got word from my church-planting coach that he had underestimated the amount of money I would need to succeed because of the slower, more meticulous approach I was taking. Instead of the $150,000 I had already raised and the $8,000 a month I was trying to raise, he said I would need closer to $750,000. I was nowhere close to that number.

And to make matters worse, I wasn't even close to hitting the number of people I needed to meet a month. Time is flying by and I'm still building a base of people, but this is slow, meticulous work. These people live extremely busy lives. They're working forty-five to fifty hours a week, living in one of the most expensive areas of the country. They have kids. They have school events. They have maybe one weekend day to spend with their family. And here I am asking them to give their time to something I'm trying to build.

I'm starting to realize: this is going to take a long time. A very long time. And I don't have the money to cover it.

Gradually, I felt more and more alone. Jula was working three twelve-hour shifts a week; she's gone completely on these days, and when she's home, it essentially takes her the same amount of time to recover from those shifts. She had to work, of course, but it accentuated my sense of isolation and vulnerability, and ultimately, she wasn't accessible anyway because our relationship had become so frayed.

Meanwhile, I'm out there every day putting myself out on a limb, living in this glass house where you feel completely naked, completely vulnerable asking people to invest themselves in this thing you're trying to create. At the same time, I'm not even close to raising enough money to keep everything afloat and it has become painfully clear just how long it will take to build the relationships I will need to form the bedrock of my church.

There are lots of reasons a church plant can fail, in the end. I would have been fine with just about any other reason than the reason I was failing. And that was money. The fear of not raising enough money was the one reason I hesitated before setting out to do this in the first place. And that was what God had assured me through Isaiah 41:10. He would have my back. I need not worry about money because He would provide.

And now? He doesn't have my back. He isn't providing. All I do is worry about money, because He was wrong: I'm running out. And there's no turning back. There's no Plan B. The money is dwindling. The amount of time it will take to make relationships is increasing. I'm spending more than I'm raising. I'm becoming more isolated.

And the clock is ticking.

My rent is $3,700 a month. I have a wife and two children to support. Bills are coming in that I can't pay.

I don't have any supports. No community. No church to fall back on. I'm living in a glass house. Now even the glass is gone. I'm naked. Everyone can see me. I'm failing.

I can't even ask Pastor Frank for support because he pushed me out.

I'm totally alone.

And then I wake up.

On a morning in August, I wake up and look at the ceiling. It's over.

My church-planting dream is over. My marriage is over. My career as a pastor is over.

Everything is over.

My relationship with God is over.

It's done. I'm done. My life is over.

The darkness began to descend again, worse than ever before. Not only could I feel it, but this time I could see it. It swirled around me. It took on the shape of little ghosts, tormenting me. I could hear voices:

You're going to die.

You're going to die.

There's nothing to live for.

I started drinking Long Island Iced Teas. Lots of them. A powerful drink. Two is enough to get you tanked. I was going on four, five of them a day. Some drink to numb themselves and to knock themselves out. I was already so numb, I was drinking so I could feel something. Anything. But I couldn't feel anything. And that's when I started telling myself: *I'm done, it's over, I'm going to kill myself.*

That's when I knew I was going to buy a gun.

Maybe two.

On August 25, I went into a gun shop and picked out a Mossberg 509A1 tactical shotgun and a SIG Sauer P-226 Scorpion handgun. I reached for my wallet to pay, but the gun salesman put up his hand and said I had to fill out some paperwork first, and he slipped me some forms.

"Sorry, man. Mandatory ten-day waiting period here in the state of California. For background checks. It's a drag, but once the waiting period is over you can come get your guns."

Ten days. Ten long, excruciating days to wait to kill myself. It was cruel. I couldn't wait that long. But what choice did I have? I filled out the forms and finalized the transaction.

On the way home, my mind was spinning. How could I sit around the house for ten days with the darkness and the voices, alone and drinking? I couldn't face it, so when I got home, I resolved I wouldn't. I would fly out to Hawaii where I had been before on vacations and wait the ten days out in Oahu. I hatched a plan to sell the trip to Jula.

"Honey, I know things haven't been working out as planned here," I began. "But listen, I just talked to a friend who's out in Oahu selling time-shares and it looks like a pretty good deal, so I'm going out there to check it out. What do you think? It would be great for you, since you can work anywhere as a nurse, and who doesn't love Hawaii?"

It was all a ruse. I had no friend selling time-shares in Hawaii. I had no intention of moving there. I just couldn't sit around in San Diego and wait ten days to kill myself.

She was concerned about how things had been going and supportive of my efforts to try to find a new place to live with better prospects for the family. With her blessing, I flew out to Oahu on the pretense of looking for a new job, but when I got there, all I did was drink until the time had passed and I could return to California and pick up the guns and end it.

I was in Hawaii from September 2 through 7. Between drinking bouts, I had two or three phone calls with Jula, keeping up the ruse that I was looking for a job and a new place to live. We talked about other possible places to live. I suggested moving to Memphis, where it's cheap and where we could recover financially, but she suggested Fresno, where her mother and stepfather lived. I said, "Sure, let's move to Fresno."

I only agreed because it would give her something to think about, so she wouldn't be thinking about me, and so I could get through the days in Hawaii and return home and get my guns.

On Labor Day, September 7, one day before my guns were available for pickup, I flew back to San Diego. Drinking alone in seclusion for days on end didn't help my state of mind: I was in an even darker place now, suspicious and paranoid. It had started back in Hawaii, fearing that someone I knew might see me out there and would guess what I was up to. What if they knew my secret, that I wasn't looking for work but drinking the days away as I waited to get the guns to kill myself? What if they contacted Jula and told her what I was up to?

As I approached my home in the rental car from the airport, I noticed cars parked in the cul-de-sac where we lived at the end of the street. There were too many cars. Why were there so many cars? Who did Jula have over? Did she know? Had someone told her? Had she found out? I could just see it: Jula opens the front door and there's a roomful of people in there, friends and family, neighbors, people I used to work with at previous churches, all standing behind her in the living room and waiting expectantly. "Honey, it's for the best," she says. My cover is blown. It's an intervention. I'm trapped.

I turn around and drive to the other side of the neighborhood where I park and call Jula.

"What's going on?" I demand.

"What do you mean?"

"Why are all those cars parked out in front of our house? Who are all those people?"

"It's just the neighbors. They're having a party and needed extra space for guests to park. I said they could park in front of our house, that's all. Is everything okay?"

Just a party. No intervention. No house full of friends and family. I felt foolish, but scared. Was I losing my grip on reality? I needed to do this. I needed to get those guns and end it before I really lost it.

"Sure, sure, honey. That's fine. I'll be right there."

When I returned, instead of opening the door to a roomful of people, I opened the door to my son Jentzen running towards me down the front hall.

"Daddy! Daddy! Daddy! I love you, Daddy!" he cried with delight, and when he reached me, he wrapped his arms around my legs and gave me a big hug.

It should have been a beautiful moment: my son saying he loves me and running down the hall to greet me after I had been away a week. But I didn't feel anything. Why didn't I feel anything? No joy? No delight? No heart melting away for my sweet, three-year-old boy greeting me at the door?

Nothing. I was numb. I drank Long Island Iced Teas to make me feel something, but the warmth of my own son hugging me only raised suspicions again. It was so unexpected, it almost felt planned to trigger something in me, something I couldn't feel.

I turned to my wife and said, "Did you tell him to do this?"

She opened her mouth and looked surprised and said no, he did that all by himself. But I still wasn't sure. I didn't know what to do with that moment of pure affection and love. I didn't know what to do with the vast difference between my son's overflowing emotions and the deep well of emptiness I harbored inside. I stumbled away and went upstairs and un-packed and went to bed with the one solace that tomorrow was Tuesday, September 8. My guns would be ready for pickup.

And on Thursday, September 10, I would kill myself.

The guns were ready. I went in to claim them, but it wasn't just in-and-out as I expected. I still had to take a handgun safety test first, which I took right there and passed. Then, the guy who was serving me asked if I wanted to shoot some practice rounds. Since I had never fired a gun before in my life, other than a BB gun when I was a kid, I took him up on the offer. He took me into the firing range and practiced with both the shotgun and handgun.

"Whoa, man," the staffer said when he saw my practice shots. "This your first time shooting, man?"

"Yeah, am I that bad?"

"No, other way around... you're really good! Good angle, good shots. Nice control. Could've fooled me! But hey, I can still give you a few tips. Why don't you first— "

"Yeah, uh, you know what? I think, not," I said, backing away. I didn't want to do this banter. I didn't want to talk to anyone. I just wanted to shoot and go. "I think I'm just going to take the guns now."

"Suit yourself! Let's go ring you up."

Back home, I hid the guns in the bedroom closet. When Thursday rolled around, Jula was already off to work and I drove the boys to kindergarten. This was the day. This was it. September 10. I knew what I would do when I got home that day, so before I left Jaxson and Jentzen at school, I kneeled down to their height and looked them in the eye so that they would pay attention and not get distracted. I said I loved them very much and gave them both a big hug. They hugged me back and said they loved me, and then they ran off to school.

I went home and started drinking, then went to the closet and pulled down the shotgun. It's the shotgun, I thought, that's how I would go. I sat in the living room and put two shells in the chamber and sat the gun on the coffee table in front of me. Where would I do this? I couldn't stomach doing it in the living room or anywhere in the house, for that matter. That would just be too horrible for Jula and the kids. Outside didn't work either. Too public. What about the garage? I decided I would do it there, but first I turned on the TV. I'll go out there in a little bit, I thought.

I drank and watched TV. I'm flipping around and land on a commercial with this woman saying, "Stay. I was made for so much more than my darkness ever wanted me to be."

A man follows. "Stay and see things change," he says.

There are others who say the same thing. "Stay," followed by why they should stay.

Text flashes on screen. It reads:

According to the World Health Organization, 800,000 people die by suicide each year.

That's one person every 40 seconds.

World Suicide Prevention Day: September 10, 2015

Seriously?! Of all the days! I couldn't kill myself on World Suicide Prevention Day. I just couldn't. There couldn't be a worse possible day to do it. I decided I had to postpone and wait until the following Thursday. I put the shotgun back in the closet.

That whole week is a blur. I did whatever I could to avoid interacting with anyone and everyone. My day consisted of getting up late, drinking Long Island Iced Teas for lunch, and picking the boys up from kindergarten in the evenings. When Jula came home at night, I handed the boys off to her and isolated myself in the bedroom and slept, and during the days I watched lots of the Republican debate coverage for the presidential election that of course Donald Trump would win.

Why did I have to wait for the following Thursday? Why couldn't I do it the day after World Suicide Prevention Day or any other day of the week? And why a Thursday? Why not a Tuesday or Wednesday? I still don't know. All I know is that it made perfect sense at the time, that I had to wait a whole week to get to the next Thursday to try again.

When Thursday finally arrived and Jula was at work and the kids at school, I got pen and paper, opened a bottle of wine, and sat down on the couch in the living room. I started drinking and began to write my suicide note, something I realized I hadn't done on my first attempt.

I can't do this anymore, it began. *I am feeling numb and dark to things. My mind is twisted. My heart is filled with pain and confusion. I hate myself. I have nothing left inside. I tried to make it, but it didn't work. I leave myself in the hands of God.*

I wrote some more, and when I finished, I decided I would also record a good-bye message on my iPhone. My mind was crowded in by darkness, I wasn't sure what words would come, but I set up the phone, pressed record, and started speaking:

I don't know what to say other than I'm sorry for the pain that I have caused.

But I can't do this anymore. I just can't.

There's nothing else. I've tried. There's nothing left in me.

You will be okay. After a few weeks you will be able to recover and get over this and you will be fine. The boys are young and they will be okay.

Just tell Jaxson and Jentzen that Daddy had a meeting with Jesus and decided not to come back.

Good-bye.

I got the shotgun out of the closet and took it out to the garage. I sat down in an aluminum, mesh-backed beach chair, rested the heel of the gun between my feet, aimed the barrel of the gun at my chest, and pulled the trigger.

Nothing.

I pulled the trigger again.

The shell popped out.

What the heck? I had loaded it correctly. Why didn't the thing go off? The gun was cocked... I pulled the trigger... and it didn't go off. I did everything right and I still did everything wrong. I couldn't even succeed at killing myself!

By this time, I was starting to feel woozy; the bottle-and-a-half of wine I had drunk was catching up with me. I must have blacked out, because the next thing I know, I'm waking up on the couch in the living room. I take out my phone: it's 4:30 in the afternoon. 4:30! That's when I'm supposed to pick the boys up from school. I got up and put the gun back in the closet. I was out of it but not drunk anymore, so I went and picked the boys up from school.

Later that night when Jula got home, I told her everything: my deepening depression, my decision to kill myself, buying the guns, the trip to Hawaii to wait out the ten-day waiting period, and my two failed attempts.

She was quiet the whole time. I could tell she was in shock. Who wouldn't be? But her silence ran deeper than that; it was the silence of someone who didn't know what to say because she didn't know me anymore. Maybe that emotional disconnect between us explains why, when I brought her to the closet in the bedroom and showed her the shotgun and pistol there, she didn't demand that they be removed from the house. Not the next day either. They stayed there for weeks.

We sat down and decided two things right there and then: one, I needed to get professional help; and two, we had to get out of there, we had to move. We had discussed Memphis and Fresno in the past and decided on Fresno. Jula's mother and stepfather lived there, so at least there would be some support. We agreed that I needed to get into an in-patient facility as soon as possible, and over the next few days we were on the phone frantically going back and forth with nearby facilities and our insurance company, trying to find a way to get me into one.

But it was impossible. What we found was that most facilities that specialize in mental health are private and generally cost $50,000 and up for a month or two of treatment. Insurance either doesn't cover the costs at all or only covers a minuscule amount of the total. There was no way to get the level of help I needed because there was no way we could ever afford such treatment.

There was no use waiting around in San Diego, then, if I wasn't going to be able to get help. We were living in a house that cost over three grand a month and we were nearly broke, so we decided to move to Fresno right away. I spent the next several weeks in a kind of zombie state. I was pretty much useless, forcing Jula to make all of the preparations for the move.

But at least with the impending move to Fresno, there was some hope, however slim, that by leaving San Diego and relocating to Fresno, I would have the time and space to recover. At least there was some sliver of hope that I could shake the darkness and move on from my failure to realize my dreams in San Diego, that I could turn my life around and start again.

CHAPTER 9

Picking Up the Pieces

Day in, day out. The same old routine. Take the kids to school, pick them up. And in between? Trump. Hillary. Fox News, MSNBC, and CNN on a loop. What crazy thing will Trump say next? Will Trump survive the *Access Hollywood* video? How will the Comey memo affect Hillary's campaign?

The nonstop coverage of the 2016 presidential election was all that kept me company between my sole duty of ferrying the kids back and forth to school. The days ground on as we settled into life at Jula's parents' place in Fresno. This was, if you re-member, where pastor Dale relocated and found jobs for Jula's mother and father. And this was where I found myself, too—unemployed, without direction, demoralized, depressed, and perpetually stationed on the couch watching the 2016 election coverage every day.

I was able to meet with Dale occasionally for coffee to break up the routine and see a friendly face, and I confided with him about how despondent I was about my failure in San Diego.

"John," he said, "look at it this way... you were doing what God told you to do. God called you and asked you to go to San Diego and you obeyed him."

"Yeah," I replied, "I obeyed him, but I didn't succeed in what he called me to do."

"It doesn't matter."

"How can success not matter when God calls you?"

"Whatever happens after God calls us is not up to us. The results of what we set out to do are not up to us. Maybe you build a church of hundreds or a few dozen or you can't establish a church at all. The key is, you heard God's call and you responded. That's all that matters, in the end. You heeded the call."

That was a hard pill to swallow. I had become fixated on why I didn't succeed, how God had assured me He had me covered with my money worries, and how money became the very thing that led to my failure. But, in the end, I knew Dale was right. I had focused too much on not raising enough money and blamed God for it. The numbers didn't matter. Hearing and acting on God's call was what mattered. And on that point, I had excelled.

Of course, when it comes down to brass tacks, money does matter. Dale knew that as well as I did. We all need money to support ourselves, our families, and, in my case, to build my church. But Dale was a good guy. He was like a big brother to me. I know he was trying his best to encourage me and get me to see the bigger picture so I could get out of the hole I was in. His message had heart. He was doing his best to help me.

Dale wasn't the only one trying to make me feel better, but he was certainly one of the more successful. Not even the therapists I saw at the time made much of a difference. In fact, they only made things worse.

It was a big step for me to go into therapy and it was long overdue. I was both nervous and hopeful when I walked into that first therapist's office. I completely unloaded. I told that therapist the whole story about my suicide attempts and my life leading up to them. I opened my heart up to him with hopes that he could help me.

When I finished telling him my story, he rubbed his chin and opened his eyes wide and said, "Whoa. Wow. You've really been through a lot, haven't you? How did you handle all of that?"

I looked at him like he was the crazy one. Of course, I had been through a lot! Why was he saying that, like I didn't already know that? And how am I "handling" it? How did he *think* I was handling it?

"That's what I'm telling you," I replied. "I'm *not* handling it. That's why I'm here. For you to *help* me handle it."

"It sounds like talking about this is upsetting you. That's understandable. Are you upset, John?"

I threw my hands up. "Are you kidding me? Of course, I'm upset!"

"Maybe you can talk about that?"

"I just did! I just talked about it for half the session!" I got up. "That's it. I'm outta here."

I left and never went back.

Strike one.

The next therapist wasn't any better. She was an older woman, very sweet and gentle, kind of grandmotherly. I gave her the spiel and she shook her head and kept murmuring about how sorry she was.

"Oh, I'm so, so sorry, John," she said. "Things will get better. In time, things will get better."

"Listen, I don't need to hear that," I said. "The fact is I'm not getting better and need help. Real help. I don't need your comfort."

"I know you're hurting, but it will take time. You have to talk it through."

"Talking is fine, but I need concrete steps, things I can do to get better. Is anyone listening to me?"

It was either this or fifty-thousand-a-month for treatment in a facility. *So, forget it,* I thought, *this isn't working, I need to find another way forward.*

I got up and left her as well.

Strikes two and three.

Therapy was out.

Things couldn't have been bleaker, but sometimes what you need comes along just at the right time. Over the years, I had kept in touch with my friend Troy Mini, who I had worked with back at Lakeland Regional Hospital. He now lived in Boston and one day talking on the phone I told him what had happened recently and how I didn't know which way to turn. Immediately, he asked if I had ever thought of becoming a chaplain.

A chaplain? What's a chaplain?

"Oh man, that would totally fit you, John," said Troy. "A chaplain is like being a pastor without all the trappings of being a pastor, the administrative and fundraising work and the community building and all that. Instead, you just get to work with people one-on-one all the time, like a spiritual guide."

All it took was this one conversation to plant the seed in my head about becoming a chaplain, a seed of hope. Maybe there was a place for me after all in the church—only, as a chaplain, I wouldn't be physically in a church, and I wouldn't be responsible for all the day-to-day worries of running a church. I would work in a facility like a medical clinic or a hospice and my flock would be patients looking for comfort.

I stuck that in my back pocket as we were inching towards the holidays. Thanksgiving was fast approaching and my brother Greg called and wanted to know if I wanted to come out to his place in Quincy, Illinois, to celebrate the holiday together with him and his wife, Debbie. They knew what was going on with me and had been texting to see how I was doing, but this was the first time Greg had reached out like this.

I said that, unfortunately, I didn't have the money to fly the family out. I could only cover about half the cost.

"Don't worry about it," said Greg. "I'll pay for half the airfare if you can pay the other half. How does that sound?"

The gesture meant a lot to me. In truth, I hadn't seen Greg and his family for about ten years and we didn't have a particularly strong relationship. But here he was making a meaningful effort to reach out and include me and my family with his for the holiday. I couldn't in good faith turn him down.

What seemed like a good idea on paper turned out to be an awful experience in reality. I was still very much in the depths of depression. I wasn't engaging with people, and over the several days at my brother's place, it showed. I would slink out of the room and sit in the den by myself and watch the news, my go-to source of comfort, while the rest of the family celebrated the holiday. There was this creeping sense all around the edges of that holiday weekend that nobody knew how to handle me. It was like everyone was trying to pretend everything was normal, when we all knew it wasn't. There was an elephant in the room and that elephant was me—or rather, I was the elephant in the *other* room, watching cable news.

This reticence from my family about my condition only made me feel worse. It became clear that they didn't know how to talk to someone who is mentally ill. They didn't know how to just be direct and up front and cut out the crap. They were tiptoeing around me. I wished we could have all sat down when I first got to their place in Quincy and just laid it all out there: things were bad. Really bad. I needed people who could help me. Instead, I found myself surrounded by people who needed to be taught how to help me. How's that for a catch-22?

Back home, I started doing some work again for a local Assemblies of God church that needed someone to come and speak every Sunday. When they asked me, my first instinct was that I wanted to say no. I didn't feel ready to stand in front of a congregation and speak again. But I also didn't feel like I should turn the opportunity down. I have always felt that when a door opens, you should walk through it, because you never know what might come of it.

I agreed to do the speaking, but it was tough. I felt like I had lost the passion and heart for it, especially when we covered the Gifts of Spirit series, which addresses the idea of opening yourself to be led by God. I opened myself to be led by God once. He led me to San Diego to plant my own church. And where did God's guidance get me? Nearly broke, drunk every day, buying guns, and attempting to take my own life, that's where. Who was I to talk about following the leadership of God? Who was I to stand in front of all these good people and talk about that? I felt like a fraud, but somehow I muscled through it. Somehow, I stood up there and gave those talks for six months.

That year was a long slog, but gradually I started to feel better. And despite the debacle of Thanksgiving at my brother's, in October 2016 I decided to organize a trip to Hawaii with me, Jula, and my two brothers and their spouses. I thought of it as a way for me to build my relationship with my brothers and to strengthen my support network. We stayed in a three-bedroom time-share for a week and, although I was still dealing with depression and didn't participate in everything, we still had a great time. What's more, I started to feel even better out there in Hawaii. My relationship with my brothers had never been stronger and I could feel I was starting to claw myself out of the ruins of the recent past. I was starting to rebuild my life. And Hawaii was an absolutely magical place, lush and vivid and real. I even turned to Jula at one point and said, "You know what? I could really see us living out here one day."

This renewed positivity stuck with me when we returned to Fresno. I still had the idea of becoming a chaplain tucked away in my back pocket ever since that conversation with Troy. Why not take a look online and see what kind of jobs are out there?

The very first search I did, I spotted an open chaplaincy position at Bristol Hospice in Hawaii. After I read the job description, I thought: *I can do that.*

They called me the day after I applied. We did a phone interview and a Skype interview and soon after they offered me the job. I had no idea my suggestion to Jula that we move to Hawaii would be realized so soon. It all happened so fast. But for the first time in what felt like forever, things were looking up.

We moved out there at the end of December 2016 and I started work in early January 2017. Hawaii did not disappoint. Our house in Oahu was perched on the side of a lush, green mountain in a neighborhood that looked down over the entire city of Honolulu and, beyond, the glittering Pacific Ocean. In the evenings, the sun set into the ocean like a giant orange slice and at night the city lights twinkled below and the stars above. We had a balcony off the house where I would sit and just watch it all. It was a place of great peace and solace for me.

And it was something I never could have expected, the hospice where I started working in my newfound role as a chaplain was also a place of solace and peace. That might sound funny coming from a guy who had recently tried to check himself out and was now working with people on the very precipice of death. But in truth, hospice work is all about solace and peace. It's all about helping patients find comfort in the final weeks and days of their lives.

That's not to say the role came naturally to me. I had never worked as a chaplain before and certainly not in a hospice. One of my first patients was a woman by the name of Bonnie. She was in the ward for people with dementia and Alzheimer's. I went in and said hello and introduced myself and she just gave me a blank look and didn't say anything. Then I motioned to the chair next to her bed.

"Do you mind if I sit here and talk with you, Bonnie?" I asked.

She gave the slightest of nods, so I sat down.

"Thanks, Bonnie," I said. "It's really nice to be here with you. I'm the chaplain here at Bristol Hospice and I'm here to talk with you if you like. Or if you want me to play some music or read to you, I'm happy to do that too. Whatever you like."

But again, she didn't say anything. She just remained quiet and kept looking at me.

Crap, I thought. *I'm lost. It's my first patient and I'm totally blowing it. Maybe this whole idea of becoming a chaplain was a mistake.*

I wasn't sure what to do or say next, but I noticed that her right hand was out and she was rubbing the fabric of the bed curtain between her thumb and index finger. I looked at her and our eyes met and then I reached out and touched the fabric and did the same thing: rubbed it between my fingers.

"That feels nice, doesn't it?" I said.

That got a smile and even a little giggle out of her.

Okay, I thought, *there's a connection.*

But her eyelids were starting to droop; she was starting to fall asleep on me.

I'm not doing that great with her if I can't connect with her on a level more meaningful than rubbing a curtain!

Finally, I decide to level with her.

"Hey, Bonnie?" I said. "Do you want me to stay or should I go?"

And she said, "Stay."

It surprised me to hear her voice at last and what she said made me feel better. I sat in the chair and she fell asleep. But now I started to doubt again. Five, ten minutes went by.

What do I do? Do I stay here? Do I leave? How long will she be asleep?

Fifteen, twenty minutes went by.

I was just starting to think of getting up when she opened her eyes. The moment she opened them, she looked over to the chair where I was still sitting. I could see a look of anticipation on her face, followed quickly by relief when her eyes met mine. That's when it hit me. All she needed was for someone to be there. That's what she needed that day. That was all. Just presence.

When I talked with the executive director later that day, I expressed concern that I wasn't sure if I had succeeded with Bonnie. But she said I had done everything perfectly.

"That's the Ministry of Presence," she said. "Sometimes it's enough to just be with someone. Sometimes, that's all anyone needs."

Turned out, it was something I needed too—just being with people who were present. All my life, I had felt invisible: unheard, unseen, and unnoticed. Turned out, I didn't necessarily need to be heard, seen, or noticed. I just needed some form of connection. Human connection. Closeness and presence. And that's exactly what I found hospice patients needed most of all in the days before they died. They needed to be close to someone. That's something very few people had been able to give me in my life up to that point, not even people who were supposed to fulfill that role—my family or my wife.

Hawaii didn't change my marriage for the better. It may have made it worse. Hawaii is such a vibrant, lively, gorgeous place. I got to be very active there, but Jula stopped participating. When I went to gatherings at friends' places or on trips to the beach, I would bring the boys along and people would ask, "Where's Jula?" I would have to make up some excuse because I couldn't say the truth, which was that she didn't want to come, she preferred to stay at home.

That was how things started going. I did a lot with the boys, just me and them. The beach. Friends' parties. Coworker gatherings. On Jentzen's fifth birthday, I took him for a hike up Diamond Head. It was his special birthday request and I impressed upon him how big of a hike it was, and that Daddy wasn't going to be picking him up and carrying him half the way. He was so excited, he hiked the whole way up and down without a problem.

I loved my job and my kids, but I also needed my alone time. After work, I started going to Lucky Strike, which is like a Dave & Busters—a restaurant, bar, and video game arcade all in one. I would go for a couple of hours to unwind and I got to know everyone there—the waiters, the bartenders, the managers, some of the other patrons. It was like my personal Cheers, where everybody knew my name. Chaplaincy work was fulfilling, but it was emotionally taxing. This was my "me" time.

When I would return home after Lucky Strike, it became clearer and clearer just how strained my relationship with Jula had become. We weren't fighting, but where was that closeness? Where was that presence? We lived in the same house, but a chasm had opened between us that was miles apart. There was no closeness. There was no presence. We were more like roommates than spouses. Just two people living together. Yes, we had the boys to take care of, but with them she had withdrawn from so many activities. I asked her several times if she wanted to join me for counseling and even suggested she get solo counseling, but every time, she demurred.

Finally, one night I came home and sat down with Jula and said, "You're so unhappy, Jula. And I'm unhappy. I know we both want what's best for the boys. But this just isn't working anymore. I think it's time to think about a divorce."

We agreed this was the best course of action. We would decide between ourselves how we wanted the divorce to go. We didn't need to go through the courts to figure it all out. We decided that the boys would be with her during the school year and would come live with me when they went on their fall, spring, and summer breaks. No alimony. No child support. I would contribute to the kids' upbringing as much as I always had. It made me feel good to know that we both agreed on all the terms and came to an amicable agreement.

Meanwhile, as my marriage was falling apart, I was loving my work as a chaplain at the hospice, which was so varied and emotionally meaningful. Working there day-in and day-out, I quickly became aware that the hospice wasn't able to adequately serve a good portion of our patients. Half of our patients at Bristol were Buddhist due to the high population of Buddhists in Hawaii, but very few of the staff had any formal training in Buddhism. If we were going to be able to fully provide comfort to our Buddhist patients, we needed to be better trained in Buddhist ways and practices.

I decided to learn more about the Buddhist faith, so I took some courses at the Buddhist Study Center at the University of Hawaii. While studying there, I ended up befriending several of the Buddhist ministers at the temple and invited one to come to Bristol to give some seminars to the staff. He came down and taught one- to three-hour seminars to the chaplains and social workers at Bristol so that everyone could provide better care to our Buddhist patients. My relationship with the ministers developed to the point that we could call a minister in to perform bedside service when someone was imminently passing. This was very meaningful to patients and their families, since none of us could officially perform a Buddhist memorial service.

My favorite memory of all working at Bristol was when a patient by the name of Harold asked me if I could help him with two requests. First, he asked if I could officiate the renewal of his vows with his wife. Of course, I could, I said. What was his second request? I was standing by his bedside with his wife by my side at the time, and they both motioned over to something by the couch. It was a large cinder block with a hole gouged out in the middle.

"What's that?" I asked.

"That's a vessel for my urn," replied Harold.

"His ashes will go in there," said his wife, pointing to the hole in the center. "And these pipes will secure it."

She motioned to some curved PVC piping attached to the hole in the block.

"Okay, and then what happens?"

"I'm hoping you can oversee my memorial service and put my urn in there," said Harold. "And then take me out to the ocean and drop me in so I can settle at the bottom of the sea floor."

Drop him in the ocean in a huge cinder block? How on earth was I supposed to manage that? Was it even legal?

I had no idea. But like everything in my life when faced with a major challenge I heard myself saying, "Of course, Harold. I'll see what I can do to make that happen. How does that sound?"

And his wife squeezed his hand and they both smiled at me.

I performed the renewal of their marriage vows—that was the easy part. When Harold passed I did exactly what he asked me to do: I dropped his ashes, housed inside a cinder block, into the Pacific. I rented out a glass-bottomed boat and hired three scuba divers to accompany about twenty of his friends and family out to a point off Waikiki and the scuba divers orchestrated the placement of the cinder block on the sea floor. As they did, I performed a memorial service. The scuba divers secured the exact coordinates of the placement of Harold's urn and gave them to his wife so that she, his family, and friends could go out there and remember him in the exact spot where his ashes lie to this day, under the rolling waves of the great Pacific. The giving of solace and comfort doesn't end with the patient; it extends to everyone he or she knew.

No matter how much experience I already had, I certainly couldn't do this work all on my own. I needed someone to bounce ideas off of and share some of the stories of working with my patients, someone who could listen and give me some guidance. That's where my great friend and mentor Clarence Liu came in. Clarence was a seventy-two-year-old former Catholic priest, born and raised in Oahu, who had been involved in hospice work for forty years. He was a veritable fountain of knowledge. We met every month at Starbucks to talk, and it was something I eagerly looked forward to, our very special meetings. I wouldn't have been able to do the work I did at Bristol, certainly not as well as I did, without his wise guidance.

I would need this guidance, because almost as soon as things had started to take an upswing in my life, signs of trouble began to threaten to dash my hopes yet again. It started in August 2017 when I got a pretty big health scare. I was experiencing periodic headaches. They weren't normal headaches, the kind I had experienced before. They were located at the back of my head, between my neck and the top of my head, a place I never really had headaches before. And then they started to get worse. One day, I got dizzy and nauseous when the headache came on. I went to the ER. They did a CAT scan and detected two lesions. Then they followed up with an MRI and found a tumor.

The neurologist diagnosed me with a small brain tumor. But it wasn't an imminent threat, he said.

"It's very small and it will only grow very slowly. Very, very little year after year. Think John McCain or Ted Kennedy. You just need to monitor it with an MRI every year. You should come back for a six-month follow-up, though."

Small comfort.

It was around this time, with my impending divorce, that I decided to try therapy again. Her name was Lisa Ho and I found her by searching Google. In our first session, I led off by telling her about my previous two therapy experiences and how I had walked out on both.

"I'm not trying to put any pressure on you," I said, "but I know I need real help here, and if I can tell this isn't working then I might just get up and walk out on you too."

She looked at me and she said, "That's okay. After a couple of sessions, I might say this isn't a good fit and maybe you will have to find you someone else."

Suffice to say, I wasn't expecting that response. It stung a little bit. Not in a bad way, but in a way that made me think I may have finally met my match. I may have met the person who could cut through my issues and get to what's really going on with me.

And she did. She helped me figure out some of my triggers for depression and how to short-circuit them. She introduced me to ways to beat back some of my anxiety. And she explored some of my relationship issues with my family. She helped me uncover a lot of layers of depression. We looked back at different events in my life, times I hadn't looked at closely in years, and worked through them. It was through her that I realized I had been struggling with depression since I was a young teenager and didn't even know it, that I have had depression my whole life.

We dealt with issues that were imminent as well, like my divorce with Jula, which was slated to be finalized by the end of December when Jula and the boys would leave for Fresno. As the week of their departure neared, it felt like a weight was slowly lifting off my neck. I know it's strange to say, but during this interim period, I actually felt good about the divorce, not because I wanted my family to break apart and my kids to leave, but because I realized my marriage to Jula was troubled deeply. My marriage to her was one of the few vestiges left of the time I spent trying to build a persona that would please my family and position me to become a pastor. Now that we were breaking up, I was one step closer to finally shedding that persona forever.

In the months before they left for California, I rented a 580-square-foot apartment and started living there and having the boys over to get them used to staying with me there. The next couple of months were so busy with moving and closing down the house, the day of my family's departure crept up on me. On Christmas Day 2017, Jula and the kids left for California. I hugged the boys good-bye and said I loved them very much and looked forward to seeing them soon. Then they left for the airport and I tended to the last of the house cleaning before the final inspection and handing the keys over to the landlord. I went back to my new apartment and just sat there and took several big, deep breaths. It was quiet. It was just me, alone, living in my own place now. The boys were gone. Jula was gone. The next time I would see Jula and the boys would be in March for the boys' spring break. I took it in, my new life, and then went about my day.

This was, in some ways, the beginning of a new era for me, a time when I could hang out with friends at Lucky Strike and not worry about going home to a wife I didn't talk to. But in other ways, this was becoming one of the darkest times in my life. Living alone, I found myself increasingly isolated. I would come home after work and go online for hours at a time, onto sites like Instagram and Tumblr and YouTube, where I quickly found content that reinforced everything I was feeling. There were countless memes that focused on dark, suicidal thoughts. They said things like:

People who die by suicide don't want to end their lives, they want to end their pain.

I smile. I try. But the truth is, I want to die.

Worthless, Pointless, Useless, Pathetic, Depressed = Me.

All the memes were fashioned in black-and-white with shadowy backgrounds or storm clouds or angry, charcoal scribbles. But my favorite meme, the one that still sticks with me, was an animated GIF of a man on the precipice of what looks like a black hole on the surface of a lake with all the water being fiercely pulled into it. The scrabbles on his hind feet and the backs of his hands trying to fight the inevitable tumble into the abyss. Because the GIF is on a loop, it just plays over and over again. The man never falls into the hole, but he's perpetually on the verge of it.

That was me. The black hole was suicide.

On YouTube, I also started watching soulful but dark and often angry music videos by R&B artists including songs with titles like "Anxiety," "Dying Inside," and "Fallen Angel." Many of them had hopeful messages, but along with the memes, they continued to feed my obsession with suicide-related content.

About a month after my family left, my brother Greg called to see how I was doing. I told him I wasn't doing that great. On top of my increasingly dark thoughts, the six-month follow-up for my brain tumor was approaching and it was weighing heavily on me.

"What can I do to help, John?"

"Well, if you really want to know, and I'll admit this up front, this is very selfish of me... but would you be able to fly out here and visit with me for a week or so?"

To my surprise, Greg said, "Sure. I think that's a good idea. Let's do that."

In February, Greg and Debbie flew out for the week of my follow-up MRI. They intentionally planned it that way so they could be with me during that week, for the MRI and the meeting with the neurologist when I would find out if indeed my tumor was slow growing or if it had grown significantly since my last MRI. Thankfully, the follow-up MRI confirmed what the neurologist had originally thought: the tumor had not grown, so it would very likely be a slow-growth tumor.

I was starting to feel close to my brother and his wife. They had really proved to me that they cared: first, inviting me to Thanksgiving; then calling to see how I was doing and flying out to support me during my second MRI. I felt close enough that I invited them to one of my therapy sessions with Lisa, just to sit and listen and be with me as a support. They came to the session, and after, I agreed to give them permission to talk with Lisa at any time to have a family member in the loop as another level of support.

March was here before I knew it, along with Jaxson and Jentzen's spring break. Jula flew them over and stayed a week in Hawaii doing her own thing with her mother while the boys stayed with me. I had no idea how hard it would be taking care of the boys on my own after being free of them for several months. It was a sign of how depressed I had become that I felt like I simply couldn't handle them anymore. Imagine a six-year-old and an eight-year-old who haven't seen their father in over two months, suddenly free from their mother, free of school, and staying with their father back in Hawaii again for two weeks. Imagine how excited those kids must be. Well, that's exactly what Jaxson and Jentzen were. They were jumping all over me wanting to do everything under the sun. They clung onto me like Saran Wrap. I loved them. I knew they missed me. I knew they were young and excited. But my anxiety level went through the roof. Several nights I cried myself to sleep because I couldn't handle the anxiety of dealing with them. But I managed to get through. This time.

The anxiety and depression I experienced when my kids visited had shaken me. When I saw my primary care physician next, I told him my meds weren't working. We had been trying various medications and so far, nothing had been very effective.

"You know, a lot of my patients with PTSD say they find relief with marijuana," he said. "Some of them use CBD and THC or a combination and it really helps them. Would you be interested in giving that a shot?"

Truth was, I had already sourced some pot from a friend and had experimented with it and found it did indeed help, so I agreed to give it a go—this time legally, with a medical marijuana card. I was new to it all, so I initially didn't use it that much. It took me some time to get over the paranoia of using it, with fears that work might randomly drug test me and find out and fire me (although later I talked to the executive director and she said it was no problem).

Meanwhile, my depression continued to deepen. In April, I hosted a party for my birthday at Lucky Strike, which turned out to be a wonderful time. Even though the party was a blast and I was enjoying my newfound freedom, when I got home that night, I found myself alone and isolated. Where was my family? Where was the life I used to have? Where were my dreams and aspirations?

I pulled out my Sig Sauer Scorpion handgun and laid it on the end table of my recliner and sat and looked at it.

When am I going to do this? When am I going to get this over with? Should it be now? Should I do it now?

Not now, I decided. Soon. But not now. Very few people knew the depths of despair I had fallen into. At work, I kept a professional persona—smiles and comfort for the patients. I'm the chaplain in a hospice. How can I be depressed when

I'm supposed to be alleviating the pain of dying people? I did tell a few coworkers that I was having a tough time. They knew about the divorce. Everyone going through a divorce has a hard time. Why was I any different?

Somehow, I made it through the spring and into June when I would look after the boys for the summer. They would be with me for about two months, from June to early August. Within the first few days of the boys staying with me, I knew I couldn't do it. I was crying myself to sleep the first few nights because they were all over me again like Saran Wrap, so excited to see me, back in Hawaii and wanting to do everything under the sun while I was trying to fight off the worst depression of my life. Sometimes, they would spin out of control and I had to leave them in the living room and go into my room and close the door and smoke some of my medical marijuana to try and get my anxiety levels down.

But medical marijuana couldn't stop what happened next. On June 30, I woke up with unbearable stomach pain. I used the bathroom and when I got off the toilet and looked down there was blood in the bowl. Lots of it. The stomach pain got unbearable. I called 911. The ambulance came and took me and the boys to the hospital where I was diagnosed with colitis. They discharged me with some medication. A coworker was able to pick us up and bring us back home, get the boys to bed, and make sure I was settled in.

I didn't know how things could get any worse. I had two boys to take care of for another month, but I couldn't do it. Mentally and physically, I was falling apart. I couldn't properly care for them. I was only giving them baths every several days. I told my therapist about it.

"I can't do this anymore. Can you help me?" I pleaded with her. "Please, can you help me here?"

"Is there someone, anyone, you can reach out to for help?" she asked. "A friend? A family member?"

That's when I thought of Greg, who had shown such concern for me over the past couple of years and who had even come out with his wife when I had my second MRI.

"Let's call him now, here, in session," suggested Lisa. "Would that be okay?"

I said yes and we got Greg on the phone.

"Greg," I said, "I'm in trouble here. I thought I could do this, but I can't. I can't handle the kids. Do you think you would be able to come out and help me?"

To my great relief, Greg said he would call Jula to let her know what was going on so she could make arrangements to get the boys.

And he did. That Sunday, Jula and Debbie showed up at my house and collected the boys. When they left, I had the very strange feeling both of great relief and tremendous guilt. I felt like a ton of bricks had been lifted off my back, but it was only to be replaced by the weight of failure. I couldn't be a pastor. I couldn't be a husband. And now I couldn't even be a father.

That's when the meme of the man slipping and sliding on the surface of the water with the great black hole of depression perpetually at risk of swallowing him up became a horrible reality. I felt myself slipping into the hole. I started watching those videos and memes incessantly. The darkness closed in and I could see the images from the computer screen all the time, even when I wasn't watching them, these ghost images swirling around me as my thoughts retraced all the failures of my past and I heard the voice again:

You're going to die.

You're going to die.

It was Wednesday, July 18. I knew I was going to die the next day. I looked at the numbers. My first attempt was September 17. That's 9/17. So, it made perfect sense that I would just reverse the numbers and die on 7/19. And 7/19 was a Thursday, which was the day I had chosen for my first attempt. It all fell into place.

That night I stayed up watching the videos with my Sig Sauer handgun by my side. At 2 a.m. I decided to do it. I locked and loaded the clip with five bullets. The gun was in my hand. I was ready to put the gun to my head and pull the trigger.

But I couldn't. I literally couldn't. My entire arm had become paralyzed. Out of nowhere, at the moment I decided to put the gun to my head and pull the trigger and end it all, I couldn't move my arm or my hand. I freaked out. So, I picked up the phone and called my friend Kevin. I explained to him the best I could that I had a gun in my hand and now couldn't move my hand or arm. Could he please come over and help me get this gun out of my hand?

"Bro, no, listen, I would help. But I got family over and it's like two-thirty in the morning. I can't just leave them here." I think he heard the desperation in my voice, because next he said, "I'll tell you what to do... do you have anyone else you can call?" I said I didn't, and he said, "All right. Just do this. Call your brother, okay? Just talk to him and I'll call the police."

I knew what the police would do when they came over. It was called a wellness check. They would check in on me to make sure I was okay and offer to take my guns. I agreed and hung up with Kevin and called my brother Greg. He stayed on the phone with me until the police arrived, which wasn't long at all. They were very kind, the police. They asked if I was okay and I told them I was getting there. They asked if I needed to go to the hospital and offered to take me there, but I refused. With my permission, they took my guns and ammunition, which they would hold for me at the police station. They told me to call them anytime if I ever needed help and then they left.

I slept the rest of that day. On Friday, I called my supervisor at work and told her what had happened.

"Oh, John, I'm so sorry," she said. "You need to go on federal medical leave, okay? You will have to come in and fill out some forms."

I went in and filled out the forms. Medical leave would give me twelve weeks of assistance, which I began receiving on July 20. That's how my time working as a chaplain at the hospice came to an end, a job that had been incredibly meaningful to me, where I had given and received comfort and solace. Now I was completely on my own. No family. No job. No coworkers. No distractions. No vocation. No calling. No comfort, and no solace. Just me, sitting in an empty apartment in Hawaii, wondering how it had all gone so wrong.

CHAPTER 10

My Daily Struggle

A few weeks after my second suicide attempt, still in the depths of depression, I spoke with my brother on the phone and he asked if I wanted to come to his place in Quincy, Illinois, for a visit. He said he would fly me over. Greg had already proved that he cared about me, and I needed family now more than ever, so I agreed and went out to stay with him and his wife for a ten-day stay. While there, I took advantage of the opportunity to look again at residential psychiatric facilities where I could get some help. Knowing the astronomical price tag associated with these places, I decided to put some calls through to people I knew with deep pockets to see if anyone would help me out with the expenses. Not surprisingly, I didn't find my guardian angel, and all the rejection only deepened my depression.

Meanwhile, the whole time I was in Quincy, my brother kept telling me I didn't need to go back to Hawaii. I could stay with them in Quincy.

"You can just stay here," he said. "It's no problem. We would be happy to help. And you can file for disability here in Illinois. You don't have to worry about going back to Hawaii and being on your own and trying to figure out how to make ends meet. Yeah, just stay here. Don't worry about it."

It was an incredibly generous gesture, but at the same time it felt less like a selfless offer and more like he was pressuring me to stay. I told him I would think about it, and I did. But Quincy? This place was out in the middle of nowhere on the border of Illinois and Missouri. Bitter cold in the winter. Thirty thousand people small. All white. Not a speck of color. Middle class, religious, and socially conservative. And here I am thinking of the place I called home: beautiful, lush, liberal, diverse, connected, cultured, and free. Everything Hawaii was, Quincy wasn't.

I wasn't ready to commit to anything, so I ended up going back to Hawaii. When I returned, I went on six-months temporary disability. Then, on Labor Day weekend, Greg called and again asked why I don't just come out and live with them?

"You're on this temporary disability, then you can go for Social Security disability and you have a place to stay. You don't have to worry about bills. You can just rest, get your therapy going, get your feet back on the ground, and just relax."

A free place to live? A place to get back on track with the support of family? Who would turn this offer down? But I was still trying to figure out why he was so insistent that I come. And it meant leaving Hawaii, of course, and moving to the middle of nowhere, with all the costs of moving to boot.

I told him to hold on and I called my friend Mike in Florida to bounce the idea off of him. I asked him if he would do me a favor and call Greg to feel it out a bit. Kind of like getting a second opinion. He agreed and called Greg and spoke with him, then called me back and said, "I think he sounds genuine, like he genuinely wants to help you." I even had my therapist, Lisa, give my brother a call, and she confirmed what Mike felt.

Person or place. That was the big decision I faced. My brother and his family, or Hawaii and the place I called home?

In the end, I chose person. I chose family. I chose relationship. Because that's who I've been all my life: someone who has chosen relationships and connections over all else. I chose to go live with my brother and his family because I believed we were building an important relationship, one that both of us had invested in.

This was no easy task. I had about two weeks to sort out my belongings, sell what I could, dump the rest, and make plans to ship my Ford Escape to Illinois. It didn't help that there was a rare tropical storm threatening Hawaii at the time. When tropical weather is infringing upon the islands with wind and downpours, no one is interested in buying furniture and all that. I ended up giving away most of my belongings, first to some friends and then to a group home for Alzheimer's patients, and finally to a family in need. That was about $12,000 worth of goods. I shipped my Ford Escape for about $2,200 and my plane ticket to Illinois cost about $800. While staying at my brother's would in theory save me money, the process of moving only put me further in the hole. At the end of the day, however, I was willing to make these sacrifices to be closer to my brother and his family and to continue to build the relationship we had starting building together as I got my feet back on the ground.

On September 24, I moved to my brother's. Twenty-one days later I would be out on the street.

What happened? Nothing terribly remarkable at first. Initially, I didn't have transportation because my Ford took a couple of weeks to ship. To get out of the house, I would walk to a nearby Starbucks every morning, just for something to do.

One day, I was asking around the staff at Starbucks if anyone knew someone who could give me a ride and that's when I met one of my few, but very important, friends in Quincy. An older man poked his head up and asked where I needed to go.

His name was Dave and he was a retired IT guy. He was happy to give me a lift and we had a good chat. After that, every time I went to Starbucks in the morning, I would sit down with Dave and we would talk over coffee. He was one of the few people I could just chew the fat with. I shared my story with him, everything from my time as a pastor to my suicide attempts. He said he was familiar with suicide; a relative had killed himself. He got it, he understood where I was coming from, and that made me feel even more at ease with him. It became my routine to go to Starbucks every morning, and Dave would always be there and we would talk, of all things, quite a bit about religion and politics. Not exactly the coziest of topics in that insular, small town. But Dave wasn't insular or small.

Apart from my connection with Dave, I didn't have much else going. I was still terribly depressed and now I was in drab Quincy, Illinois, without a car and without anything to do. I couldn't stay at Starbucks all day, so I did a lot of what I did back in Hawaii—watched TV and slept a lot. There was also a Buffalo Wild Wings in town and I thought, since it's a sports bar, it could be a place where I could hang out and meet some people, like Lucky Strike in Hawaii. Since I felt so out of my element everywhere else in town, I thought it could be a place where I could feel more comfortable.

I stepped into Buffalo Wild Wings and was hit with a wall of white America. Everyone, from customers to servers to kitchen help, was white. There wasn't a single person of color to be found. This was Republican country. Social conservatism ruled. Diversity did not. Among the patrons, I saw my fair share of MAGA hats and heard my fair share of racist comments. But this was what I had. I wasn't comfortable there, but at the very least it was a place to go to get out of my brother's house.

Two weeks into my stay at my brother's, I was sitting at the kitchen table talking to Greg. I was telling him about how I was doing emotionally and the importance of staying somewhere I felt mentally and physically safe. Debbie was washing some dishes and suddenly she jumped in.

"You know, John, it's important to own your feelings," she said. "You can't keep trying to find safe places to hide out."

Her comment rubbed me the wrong way. Owning my feelings wasn't the issue. The issue was that I was suffering from a deep depression and needed help and she couldn't expect everything to be normal and "owned up" when someone in my condition with suicidal ideation was living in her home.

"Sorry, but I'm not talking to you, Debbie," I said. "I'm talking to my brother."

She gave me a sour look and turned back to the dishes.

Perhaps that small argument presaged what was to come, but in truth, nothing could prepare me for what happened next.

On Monday, October 15, I got a text from my brother asking me if we could meet. I figured he wanted to tell me that he was flying out to be with his wife, who was in Pennsylvania at the time because her mother had just passed away. At ten to six, he walked in the door and I told him I was happy to chat and afterwards I was heading to Buffalo Wild Wings to watch the Packers play the 49ers.

"Well, just hold on there a minute, okay?" he said.

"All right, no problem, I'm here," I said. "What is it you need to tell me?"

"Just wait, okay? I have a few people coming over."

"What do you mean? Who's coming over?"

"Just wait, okay?"

The doorbell rang and in came seven guys, one by one, and Greg had everyone sit around the kitchen table and I still had no idea what this was about, but it didn't feel good at all.

"John," said Greg. "These are my friends and they support me and this is what I have to say. First, I think you're misdiagnosed. Second, we love you and support you, but you can't stay here anymore. Three, we got you a hotel room for tonight."

"Wait, what? What are you talking about?" I said, and I looked from face to face staring back at me, emotionless. When no one said anything, I said, "This is crazy. I didn't do anything wrong. I wasn't even planning on coming out here. He *asked* me to come. So I came. It cost me eighteen grand to make this happen... to come out here. I've only been here... what... twenty-one days? Three weeks?" I turned to my brother. "And you're kicking me out? Are you serious?"

"Those were the three things I had to say," Greg said firmly.

"Forget this, I'm leaving. I'm going to watch the game. I can't make any sense of this. I'll take care of this later."

At Buffalo Wild Wings, I was drinking a much-needed beer and watching the game when two of the men from the house came up to me.

"This is from Greg," said one, and he gave me a key and a receipt. "This is a key to the storage locker where you will find your belongings... and the receipt for the storage." Then he gave me another key. "And this is the key to the motel room where you can stay tonight." Then they stayed to talk to me for a little while.

I felt about as numb emotionally as that bitter October night. It was 22 degrees, the ground frozen solid, with sheets of snow and ice everywhere. Quincy, Illinois, in October was a lot different from Oahu in October. I went to the hotel room my brother got for me and slept there that night and the next day asked at the front desk if I could stay another night. They said no, the whole place was booked. I drove around to three nearby towns and all the hotels were full up. There must have been some local event going on; these towns were small and it was unusual all the hotels should be booked. I even went to the Salvation Army and they were full too. I asked if they had any recommendations and they told me of a place called the Althoff Hotel, just outside of Quincy. It was my last resort, so I drove over. When I walked into the front office, I saw a painted wooden cutout of palm trees affixed to the wall. Below it was a long, framed photograph of Honolulu taken from the bay. And below that, on a mantle, stood another wooden cutout that formed the word "Aloha." As it turned out, the wife of the owner of the hotel was Hawaiian, the only Hawaiian in Quincy. It felt like I was meant to stay here, and indeed I was: they had a room for me. Thank God they did or I would have frozen to death that very night.

I had no idea at the time, but this hotel room would become my temporary home for the next four months. This was my life now. But what kind of life was it? I was completely out of my element in Quincy and now my brother had thrown me out of his house. I felt like a fish flopping around on the sand. Only Quincy didn't have any sand. It had snow and ice. So I was a fish flopping around on snow and ice. Even worse! The point is, I was trying to survive from day to day, minute to minute, with everything, all odds, working against me. It was the closest I've come to hell on Earth.

Financially, like so many other times in my life, the clock was ticking. My six months of disability would run out on January 1, and here it was late October. Two months left. I decided I might as well just stay on at the Althoff until my money ran out. Meanwhile, I could start trying to raise money from anyone I knew. I didn't have any other plan. I was just trying not to suffocate out there all by myself, flopping about on the cold, dry land.

But financial concerns paled in comparison to what I was feeling inside. If I had had an easy means to kill myself, I most likely would have, but my guns were locked up back in Hawaii. I couldn't make sense of what had happened with my brother. Nothing about it made sense. Why, after all the goodwill he had shown me, after paying for me to visit him twice, after asking me, pressuring me, many times to come live with them, did he suddenly just up and throw me out? Just like that? Out of the blue? I was completely blindsided. The betrayal and rejection devastated me. It couldn't have hurt any more if he had blindfolded me, beat me with a baseball bat, and left me for dead.

I was in terrible shape and I knew it. That was my only defense: at least I knew I was in a bad way. I told my best friend Mike, "Hey buddy, listen, we're going to have to talk every day because right now I'm living in the darkest place I've ever been and I'm ready to just check out." He was there for me, as was my friend Bill in California, who I also spoke with during this time.

Complicating matters was the fact that I didn't have access to the one thing that dramatically helped me with my depression: marijuana. When I moved to Quincy, one of the first things I did was apply for a medical marijuana card. They said it would take around thirty days for the approval to work its way through the system, but in reality it ended up taking 101 days. For more than three months, I was without one of the greatest weapons in my arsenal against falling into a suicidal depression. As a stopgap, I ended up sourcing marijuana off the street. A maid at the hotel turned out to be one of my most reliable dealers and there was the added benefit that she could bring it right to my room. But street weed isn't the same as medical weed. The strains and strength vary tremendously, so it only went so far in helping me and I remained in a very dark place.

At least I stuck to a daily routine, rudimentary as it may have been. At 8:00, I got up so I could get to Starbucks by 8:30 or 9:00 where I would meet with Dave and we would chat until about 10:30. Then I would head over to the soup kitchen at Horizons until lunchtime where I had started going to for lunch to save money. Doors didn't open until noon, but I learned pretty quickly that you had to get there early and get in line. If you didn't, the best pickings might be gone by the time you got to the serving line. Of course, I got to know some of the other patrons of the soup kitchen and heard a lot of sad stories. Broken families, broken lives, broken dreams. Drug and alcohol addiction. People abused and demoralized and at the end of their rope. And there I was, breaking bread with them every day. My dreams had also been broken, my family, and my life. I too was demoralized and at the end of my rope. After lunch, there was a table in back with some food you could take with you. I took whatever I could reasonably carry so I could have something for dinner.

Lunch was over at 12:30. From there I might go to the post office to pick up mail or I might have a therapy session with the psychiatrist I had started seeing in Quincy who helped me apply for my medical marijuana card. But if I didn't have therapy, my day was basically over at about 1 p.m. That left a good portion of the day open and unstructured, which led to the kind of rumination and feelings of failure that only made my depression worse.

Even though I was depressed, it didn't change the fact that I'm a sociable person. That may have been my saving grace. It seemed like every time I might have fallen into the dark hole, there was someone there to take my hand and say, "No, hold on." Buffalo Wild Wings may have been full of conservative white people, but that didn't frighten off Kaitlyn and Allison, a lesbian couple I met there one night and quickly hit it off with. The three of us ended up hanging out at Buffalo Wild Wings. Sometimes we would find a quiet corner to smoke a joint, head to Tangerine Bowling Alleys to knock down some pins, or take in a nightclub every now and then. I never told them very much about my circumstances, but I didn't have to for them to be a huge support for me. Who would have thought: in the middle of white conservative America, in MAGA country, that the people who show me the most love and compassion, who befriend me unconditionally, who open their arms to me when my own brother threw me out of the house for no apparent reason, would be two lesbians. To me, they were two sparkling guardian angels who many people in that town would have called just the opposite. Between them and Dave, I was just able to keep from suffocating as I fought to stay alive.

But depression has a mind of its own. Even though I was seeing a psychiatrist and taking medication and had these three lovely people for support, my depression was only getting worse. And then the holidays rolled around. Christmas and

New Year's, a time of year when you're supposed to be with family and the comforts of home. And here I was: I hadn't heard from Jula this whole time since she took the kids back, I was living alone in a hotel room, I didn't have a job, barely any money, and my brother had thrown me out of his house. Thank God I had a few friends, but I was slipping further into that dark hole. That meme of the man trying to keep from being swept into that black hole kept replaying in my mind. I was nearly over the edge.

This was when I went out to a hardware store and bought some rope. Back at the room, I tied a noose. I watched YouTube to learn how to tie it. After doing some research, I had learned that this was a good way to go if you didn't have a gun or other means. The intention wasn't to hang myself right there and then. The intention was to have a means of escape if I needed it at a moment's notice. I put the noose in my suitcase. If things got too bad, I would have it close by.

The holidays came and went and I made it through somehow. In late January, I was in my room texting with my brother Pete. We didn't have a deep relationship, but we would text occasionally, usually about sports. Once he even told me that he didn't want to talk with me because I probably have other people to talk with. And I said that didn't make sense, he was my brother, I definitely wanted to talk with him. But it was clear that he didn't want to hear it. There wasn't much to say about that.

That night when he texted me about sports, I texted him back: *Man, don't you want to hear about me? Don't you want to know how I'm doing?* And he said: *Yeah, sure, sure, what's up?* And I said: *You know what? I don't trust you anymore.* He said: *Why?* Pete was a strict social conservative with the Assemblies of God Church. He was so radical, he believed that if you drank, you would go to hell. So I said: *I've heard you say that if you drink a beer you go to hell. Guess what I'm doing now? I'm drinking a beer. So I guess you think I'm going to hell. That's why I don't trust you.*

There was a long pause.

Then he texted back: *Good night, John.*

Here it was. My last family member rejecting me. I opened my suitcase and pulled out the noose. *This is it*, I thought. *I'm doing this tonight.*

My brother texted his parting message at 5:22 p.m.

At 5:23, I heard my phone vibrate. Another text. Only this time, it was from the maid who sold me my marijuana.

Are you okay? You want to hang out?

I couldn't believe it. Exactly one minute after my brother texted and I went and grabbed the noose, the maid was texting me asking me if I'm all right and if I wanted to hang. I told her, sure, and she came up from the front office and we hung out just long enough to calm me down. She gave me a little pot before she left because she knew I was in a bad way and needed it. And that was that. I put the noose away for the night. Call it what you will. Divine intervention? A freak coincidence? One minute after my brother's text, possibly one minute before I could have been hanging from a noose, she texts and changes the course of everything. Call it happenstance. Call it God. Call it what you will. I call it awesome.

It was January now and that was the month my disability ended. The first week of January I got my last check. The rent for the hotel room was $800 a month. Not a bad deal, all in all. But without disability, I would run out of money fast. So I hustled. I started calling pastor friends of mine to ask if their church had benevolence funds or something to help me. Something. Anything. Maybe enough to cover a week or two of rent. But the answer I got back repeatedly was *No, no, no.* It was a horrible feeling getting rejected so many times on top of all the rejection I had already faced, and by some of the very people who should care, who should show compassion. Some of the pastors were suspicious: what did I do that caused me to be put in this situation? Through their words and tone, I could feel them pointing their fingers at me. Others said, *Well, I think you need to go to your family for help. You shouldn't be asking around. Your family should help.* They were right. Family should help. But how could I even begin to explain to them how wrong they were about my situation?

Despite all the rejection, I was able to cobble together enough money, about $4,000 a month, to cover my expenses. Some people did come through. A little here, a little there. Enough to get me through to March 1, at least. I went on food stamps, which helped, and kept going to the soup kitchen. A huge disappointment was that I was denied Social Security disability in February. I met with a disability lawyer and when I asked him if I should appeal, he gave me a sorry look. It would take at least two years, he said, before I would even see a judge. He told me the path to disability. It included checking myself into psychiatric hospitals twice a year and doing all sorts of stuff to gain the system. I thanked him and got up and left. No way, no how. My life may have been tough, but living the kind of life he depicted had to be worse.

March first came and I was broke. I couldn't pay for my room anymore. They gave me two weeks free and then I had to be out on the 15th. About a week later, I was at my wit's end. *Maybe I'll end it now,* I thought. *Maybe this is the end of the road.* I truly had nowhere to go. The next morning, I went to Starbucks as I always did. I didn't want to go, but I went anyway. It had become a habit. And Dave would be there. At least there was that.

"How did it go with the disability lawyer?" Dave asked when I sat down.

And I told him how long the lawyer said it would take for my appeal to go through the court system and all the terrible things I would have to do to prove to the state that I deserved disability.

Dave sat back in his chair and looked thoughtfully at me for a moment. Then he said, "I suppose you're wanting to get back to beautiful Hawaii about now, aren't you?"

I said, "Yeah, sure, man, of course I am."

He sat up in his seat and opened up his laptop and began typing away.

"Well then, when do you want to go?" he asked.

"What do you mean?"

"When do you want to go to Hawaii? I'll buy you a ticket there. Just let me know when you want to go and it's yours."

I could hardly believe my ears. I had never realistically thought of going back because I hardly had a cent left to my name. But now that he was offering to buy me a ticket, it seemed like a lot better place to be broke than Quincy, Illinois.

"Jeez, are you serious?"

"Of course I am. I want to do this for you."

I accepted.

Before I saw Dave for the last time, he took me aside and told me, "John, if you feel like the day is out of whack and you can't handle it anymore, just tell yourself you can always do it tomorrow."

That stuck with me. I repeat that to myself a lot now. I can always do it tomorrow. Just not today. Always tomorrow.

On March 12, I took one last look at the gray, wintry wasteland of Quincy and was on a plane back to Hawaii. Dave even paid for my truck to be delivered to Hawaii. Before I left, I didn't have any place lined up to stay. I contacted my old friend and work associate from the hospice, Larry Grimm, to ask him if I could crash at his place for a while. We called Larry the "Grim Reaper" back when I worked at the hospice, a kind of dark, inside joke, but he was anything but a scary guy. He said sure, I could stay in the spare room at his place for a while until I got my bearings. It was kindnesses like this that kept me going.

I arrived back in Honolulu with twenty-eight cents to my name. One of the first things I did was file for Social Security disability since it takes months to get a decision. On the advice of my case manager, I filed for food stamps and cash assistance, which came to a whopping $350 a month in food stamps and $388 cash assistance. It doesn't go far, but it's something. Needless to say, with so little money, I wasn't able to go out and do much. Besides, I ended up having to sell my truck since the monthly payments were more than my monthly cash assistance. That made me beholden to public transportation, for which I got a disability bus pass, but to this day I have only used it once. My depression and anxiety made it difficult for me to negotiate the schedules and transfers, the timing and the crowds of people. Mostly, my routine consisted of watching news channels and sports, but I did spend a good deal of time outdoors enjoying the sun and warmth, which I had missed so much during those dark, cold days in Illinois. At least I was back in gorgeous, colorful, vibrant Hawaii, where merely stepping outside and feeling the sun on my face could brighten me up.

I am grateful to Larry, my guardian angel, for opening his apartment to me. I had no place to go and only twenty-eight cents in my pocket when I arrived in Hawaii on Tuesday, March 12, 2019. Initially, Larry was going to charge me $450 a month to stay in his spare room. But at the time, I could not find a job; my depression was holding me back. Larry graciously told me that I could stay with him even though I could not pay.

Over time, the apartment became a safe place for me to begin the healing and recovery process. Along with the apartment, weekly therapy and regular appointments with my psychiatrist have played a role in my healing and recovery journey. I spent a great deal of time reflecting on my life. Many nights, I would cry myself to sleep battling depression and suicidal ideation.

Larry and I would have conversations on the lanai. He brought a couple of chairs out there and we named them the "chill chairs." Our conversations were mostly small talk but I still found it encouraging to be able to talk things out with someone.

We would go to Zippy's (which is like Denny's) every Saturday morning for brunch. It was a great way for us to build a trusting relationship and to check in with how things were going. Sometimes we would go to Magic Island to watch the beautiful Hawaii sunset. This always felt so peaceful to me.

I wouldn't say that I'm healed and recovered, but I am headed in the right direction. As I continue to pray and trust God, I will follow Him as He helps me.

In order for me to heal and recover, I needed to forgive my brother Greg. Even though he kicked me out of his house, I need to forgive him because God has forgiven me. I forgive my brother Greg, and now I am working on letting it go.

Something else helped brighten me up about two weeks after I returned. Another friend and former coworker from hospice, Jomel, told me about a series of seminars called PSI, a personal success and development training, that would be hosted at a nearby hotel. He encouraged me to go, but he knew I wouldn't be able to afford the $800 price tag for three ten-hour days of training. It happens that the training was on sale for $500 that weekend, he informed me, and if I could swing half the price, he would match that. Again, it's people like Jomel, people who put their money where their mouth is and truly followed through, who kept me going.

The training turned out to be a very powerful experience for me. It gave me a safe place to be vulnerable and to share some of my story with the other participants. Most importantly, talking with the other participants and getting their positive feedback affirmed my thoughts about starting a creative project, one that would prove therapeutic and help me make sense of my life. For many months, I had been thinking about writing a book about my experiences, but as usual, life got in the way, as well as my own doubts, and I hadn't written a word yet. But after my experience at PSI, it was clear to me: come hell or high water, I was going to write this book. It would, from that point forward, be the number one priority in my life. And as I sit here writing this now, so it remains.

Why? Why, then, am I telling you this story? Why am I even still here? As a depressive with suicidal ideation, this question isn't merely a philosophical exercise. This question is a daily reality. It's life or death. Here I am living out of a room in a friend's home, living off welfare and food stamps, unable to even take a bus to leave the house. My ex-wife and kids live thousands of miles away. I FaceTime with my sons every weekend, but it's not the same as being with them. I miss them so much, but every day I'm struggling with the threat of the dam breaking and releasing a flood of suicidal thoughts as it has so many times before.

And then this happened: on a Tuesday in July, I picked up the phone and called my brother Pete. My mother had taken a bad fall one week earlier and was in the hospital, so I wanted to check in and see how things were going with her. My sister-in-law picked up. I asked her how my mother was doing and she said that she was sorry, she had died two days ago. I couldn't believe what I was hearing. What was she talking about? She handed the phone off to my brother Pete and he confirmed it; she had died two days ago. Why didn't anyone call me? Pete said Greg told him no one should tell me and that our father apparently didn't want me to know. Well, what about the memorial service, surely, I can still make it for that? No, said Pete, they had just held the memorial service that very morning. I hung up the phone and slumped back in the chair. My own mother, and my family couldn't even tell me she had died. They robbed me of my chance to mourn her death. Who does this? Who treats their brother and son like this?

Why, then, don't I just do it? Why don't I just kill myself? What's stopping me? Why don't I just end this pain and the stigma of going about with an illness that people do not see, do not recognize or understand, and many who do not want to understand. When I returned to Hawaii, I went in to get my latest MRI results for my brain tumor and as the doctor pulled up the results he asked, "So, Mr. Miller, what do you do for a living?"

"Actually, I'm unemployed right now and waiting to hear back about Social Security disability," I replied.

He looked away from his computer screen for a moment and gave me a kind of up-and-down look. "Really! Well, you look fine to me!" And then he turned his attention back to his computer screen.

Later, I met with a pastor. I told him my situation and asked him if he would help me raise some personal funds just so I could get by for a little bit. His answer?

"Well, can't you just go pick up a broom and sweep?"

These are just a few examples of people assuming they understand how someone is doing simply by appearances. But depression, anxiety, and suicidal ideation don't have an appearance. You can't see them. You're not in a wheelchair. You don't necessarily look sick. In many ways, my illness, as it is with so many others struggling with it, is invisible.

This is my way of making the invisible visible. I think of Bill Wilson, founder of Alcoholics Anonymous. He went in and out of treatment but would always relapse until one day he greeted someone with the iconic saying, "Hello, I'm Bill and I'm an alcoholic." That moment caused him to be strong enough to not need to drink again. Anytime he would meet someone and say that introduction, he noticed he didn't need a drink that day and he got stronger.

I'm not about to go around shaking people's hands and saying, "Hello, I'm John and I'm a depressed man with suicidal ideation." But I can write a book that says that and more. I can make the invisible visible by telling my story. This book has the potential to reach people who are struggling with the same illness, who also feel invisible and misunderstood, and who need to hear that they are not alone. This book could also reach people who do not struggle with depression, but who most certainly know someone who is: a coworker, a friend, a family member, a student. It could remind them that not all illnesses can be seen, that we can never assume to know what someone is enduring inside, that very real pain and affliction can, and does, hide in plain sight every day.

CHAPTER 11

The Final Stretch

After living with my brother, Pete, and his wife, Pam, for nine months, I was able to save enough money and gain enough confidence to move out on my own. In January of 2021, I began researching cities all over trying to find a place that had the best options for me. I knew I would need a reasonable cost of living, and access to qualified psychologists and psychiatrists, and not be too far from my boys. Then, Jula suggested the perfect fit - Springfield, Missouri. I immediately began making plans.

I'll always be exponentially grateful for my brother, Pete, and his wife, Pam, for being gracious enough to let me stay in their home while I got my feet under me. I doubt they'll ever understand exactly what a massive impact that had on my life.

Finally, the time had come. On the third weekend of March, I packed up my things, loaded up my car, said my good-byes and thank yous, and I left for a new adventure. I drove away from Cleveland, Ohio with a wonderfully thankful and hopeful heart.

Once I arrived in Springfield, Missouri, I stayed in a hotel for one night to ensure that I got a superb night's rest. I knew I didn't have any furniture in my new apartment and sleeping on the floor doesn't exactly promise a dreamy deep slumber. Upon waking, I was more ready than ever to begin this new chapter.

Moving back to Springfield, Missouri was quite nostalgic as I had lived here twenty years ago. The community seemed familiar, even though so many things had changed. For example, Zio's was this delicious Italian restaurant that was packed to the brim all the time and was now closed. But, I was hopeful that this would be a great place to start a new foundation - especially since it has a more affordable cost of living compared to the rest of the country.

When I finally arrived at my two bedroom apartment, I was on cloud nine. I was completely ecstatic to have a place to call my own. Some would've looked at the apartments and said, "Why are you staying there? There's a lot of police activity!"

But I didn't care, in my mind I had just made heaven. I parked my Ford Escape and walked into my new space with nothing but two suitcases and a couple boxes. I knew I would need to purchase some furniture, but for now I just wanted to soak up the feeling of being home.

My home.

Later that week, I excitedly headed to a local furniture store. I found one of their cheapest bedroom sets, a bed frame and mattress, as well as a living room set, a couch, chair, a few end tables, and a coffee table. Again, I was bursting at the seams to not only have a place of my own but now to get some furniture! I could hardly stand it.

I sat down with the salesman to see if I qualified for monthly payments. I figured I would just pay the minimum monthly payment and be all set. The salesman tinkered with the computer for a moment and then slowly walked back to me.

"I'm sorry, John. Unfortunately, you don't qualify based on your current credit score."

My heart sank. What would I do now? I am so overjoyed with my apartment, but I needed furniture. I had some money built up because of Social Security backpay, but that was going to be used to cover my rent for the next few months. I couldn't give that up.

So, I picked up the phone and called my dad. I explained the situation and asked if he would be willing to put some money towards the sets. Graciously, he agreed and again I was back on cloud nine. He ended up paying for just over half of the bill and I happily forwarded my stimulus check to him as my payment. Thankfulness flowed from my heart to my dad. I couldn't have filled my apartment without him. A place of my own, furniture to fill it, and now to focus on the most important part - my boys.

I can't describe how much it meant to me that Jula and I agreed to move to the Springfield area. For the first time in years, this put me in the same town as my boys. No more flights back and forth. They were now only a short drive away. Is cloud ten an option? Because I think I found it.

The next and more important thing on the agenda now was rebuilding my connection with my boys. However, that's when those darker thoughts started creeping back in. When I had left, the boys were at their pivotal ages - five and seven years old.

How badly would my three year absence affect our relationship?
What if they reject me?
What if they don't want me around?
What if they don't want to hug me?
What if they have anger towards me?
Would they understand if I told them why?
How would I react to their reactions?

I'm already stressed and anxious just trying to get started, but what if I make it worse? Those thoughts haunted the back of my mind, but I knew I needed to be there for them now. Therefore, I put my work boots on and got to it. Luckily, it only took a few weeks before my boys were all over me just like they had been before. This helped settle my mind a bit. I wanted to keep the momentum going and keep working on our relationship. Without a drop of hesitation, I planned some things for us to do together.

Quality time is the building blocks to healthy relationships.

We had all gone fishing back in Hawaii and liked it. So, I figured we'd give it a go here too. In June, I found a place, Rutledge-Wilson Farm Park. You pay a small fee and can rent the gear right there at the Visitors Center even if you don't have a fishing license. They have a catch-and-release policy which was fine since we weren't planning on keeping any of the fish anyway.

The day finally came and off we went on our fishing adventure. I put all the worms on the hooks as Jentzen and Jaxson were absolutely not interested in doing it. We had a lot of fun, and actually caught some sun fish, but it was obvious that the boys weren't eagerly planning their next fishing trip.

Since I didn't have two little fishermen, I thought we could give bowling a try. It's a great pass time that gives you something to do but also allows you to have a conversation with those around you. Turns out, we all really enjoyed it. The boys filled the alleys with laughter and my heart with warmth. We continued to bowl for pretty much the whole summer.

My apartment had a pool that was close to my building. Along with bowling, this too became a favorite. The boys had taken swimming lessons in Hawaii when they were younger and they did fantastic, but they were still a little hesitant about putting their head under water. But we didn't let that stop our fun. We spent hours throwing a ball, using masks and snorkels, and obviously a lot of splashing - especially with squirt guns.

In January of 2022, Jentzen had begun to express interest in a new activity. I was happy to see him open up at the chance to try something different and meet new people.

"I want to do MMA," stated Jentzen to Jula. She told him that he needed to speak with me about it.

After hearing his pitch, I replied, "Really? Alright, then let's investigate to make sure you really like it." I pulled up some Brazilian Jiu Jitsu videos. I was already familiar with this form of Martial Arts thanks to Robert and my time in Olympia. After a few videos Jentzen continued, "Dad, I want to do it."

I was ready to go with Jentzen on this new adventure as I was more concerned about my relationship with him than I was with Jaxson. Both Jula and I felt like he harbored a lot of anger and frustration because of the divorce. I wanted to ensure that I spent extra time with him to help him heal those wounds as best as I could.

So, I spoke with Jula and she found one close to her workplace. It wasn't long before we had the opportunity to go and watch a class. His attention was fixed on the powerful moves, stances, and people in the room the entire time. Immediately after class ended he stated, "I'm ready to do this." Naturally, I signed him up that night. I knew that this would be beneficial in our lives in multiple ways: It would be something we could do year round to continue rebuilding our relationship, he could see firsthand the benefits of self discipline, as well as learn to defend himself.

It worked. We had weekly practices that I was able to attend. Naturally, the continuous attendance, support, cheering, and encouraging him in his new adventure had a positive result. Brazilian Jiu Jitsu was an interest we both shared and could continue to explore together. Our relationship was getting stronger, his anger towards me seemed to subside, and I couldn't be prouder of him. After receiving four white stripes and a couple silver tournament medals, he fell in love with the sport and continues to participate to this day.

Now, I needed to find something that Jaxson and I could do together. I thought he might be interested in golf because it's a good physical activity with the opportunity for quality time. Now mind you, he had never seen golf let alone had held a club before. So, the summer of 2022 we gave it a go. We got him a nice set of golf clubs and we would be on a course at least twice a week. One visit during the week, we would work on hitting the golf balls on the driving range. The other visit, we would practice chipping and putting. Every once and a while we would play the Par 3 course - he definitely beat me a couple of times. We had fun all summer long. Our goal was for him to learn the game in one summer. Sure enough, he conquered his goal all while giving the two of us something to continue to positively build our relationship.

As awesome as all of the time I was getting with my boys was, I was experiencing panic attacks, nightmares, and extreme stress. The weight seemed to be settling back in. I would wake up in the middle of many nights drenched in sweat after having full on punching and kicking fights with my bed. Unfortunately, this is something that I struggle with to this day.

It was extremely difficult for me to handle my boys. They are great kids, but they have a high and intense energy level that triggers my anxiety. I became over-stimulated and without time to reset and rest, I began to see changes in myself. became constantly overwhelmed and easily irritated over, what I would consider, silly things. The combination of working through my own things and the change in environment when my boys were over put me constantly on edge. It was exhausting.

Unfortunately, it didn't take long before my depression and suicidal ideation to come back. The thoughts are so dark. They feel like black bats circling and nipping at me. At the same time, I would hear threatening voices telling me to kill myself and other paintful things. I knew it was time and I began the search for a psychiatrist and therapist.

It was easy to find a psychiatrist. A quick review of my current medications, a few changes made, and I was all set in that department. However, finding a therapist was a whole different story. Call after call after call, the answers were all the same. "Sorry, we don't have any openings." Last, but not least, I gave Burrell Behavioral Health a call. They gave me the option to be put on a waiting list. I thought, "Well, surely it can't take but maybe a month or two." So, I agreed and began my wait. Little did I know, I wouldn't receive that call until eleven and a half months later.

Meraciously, I received a phone call from the Burrell therapist's receptionist. The lady on the other end of the phone introduced herself then asked, "Mr. Miller, are you still wanting therapy services?"

I quickly replied, " Yes, please. Why did it take so long to get this call from you?" I was shocked to hear from them. There had been absolutely no communication from them since my first conversation to get my name on the waiting list.

"With COVID, it has affected how many therapists are available." she responded.

I didn't understand her answer. However, I was so thankful that I could begin to schedule my therapy sessions. And I sure did.

My first session, I was nervous as all get out. With my history of therapy, I knew exactly what I needed, and didn't need, in a therapist. Where would this one fall? If it didn't work out, would I have to wait another eleven months? What effects would that have on my mental health? I couldn't have that. So, I decided I was going to have to stick with this situation the best that I could until they told me there were openings all over the place.

As I sat anxiously in the waiting room, I noticed a sign on the desk that said, "If it's ten minutes past your appointment, please let us know." I checked the time. It was 9:10am on the dot. My appointment was supposed to start at 9:00am. So, I walked up to the counter. I explained the situation. The receptionist thanked me and then let me know that he would page my therapist. I smiled and walked back to my seat. His help was so kind, but I couldn't help but wonder what effect this was going to have on my relationship with my therapist. Would it upset them that I called them out for being late? Before long, my therapist showed up.

It wasn't long after we had sat down, introduced ourselves, that I began communicating my expectations. I was very open about expressing that if there wasn't a connection, I would be seeking out another counselor. I didn't want to waste my time nor the therapist's time. Luckily, it has worked out well. I have learned a lot being in therapy and I'm sure I will continue to learn a lot. It is essential to my well-being and I will continue to stick with it - even though my therapist has continued to be ten to fifteen minutes late for every session.

CHAPTER 12

Tomorrow and the Four C's

I've spent a lot of time thinking and contemplating my ups, my downs, my life, my story. Honestly, just trying to figure everything out. There's something from my 2014 doctoral project that I have kept coming back to. My project was based on four ways to help a church grow or a leader to grow. After thumbing through it a few times, I realized that these strategies could be adapted to my everyday life. So, I have dubbed them "The Four C's to a Healthy Life" and they are: Community, Calling, Conversation, and Cultivation.

Community is a must. Now, this word can seem daunting. We use the word "community" for entire cities, but that's not the sense of the word that I'm talking about. Community is all about relationships - family, friendships, small groups, etc. It is finding one person at a time that knows the true version of you, cares for you, and supports you. After a while, you'll have a team of people that are on the sidelines cheering you on or sitting across the table holding your hand through your darkest nights. It is imperative for your mental and spiritual health to feel connected to others and find a sense of belonging. Without this, you are undoubtedly setting yourself up to experience more anxiety and depression.

In order to have a community in your life you have to be willing to open yourself up to relationships. It is imperative that you don't isolate yourself. You can't stay home all the time. You can't watch T.V. all the time. You can't spend hours scrolling on social media. Although in all transparency, I'm guilty of each of those things - but they did me no favors in my healing.

For example, when I first moved back to Springfield, I knew that I couldn't just stay in my apartment. I needed to get out and meet people. Soon, I met one of my neighbors, Paco. Paco has a rough background. He was in jail for many years for murder and gang banging in Chicago. However, he had turned over a new leaf. We got to know each other better, had conversations about life, spent time together, watched football or fights, and shared meals together at his place and mine. He might just be one person, but he is my first step at building my community. My team. My support system.

But it doesn't always come as easy. I met another couple, Chris and Madison, who were also my neighbors. They have a few kids together. I spent time getting to know them and they are just really good people - so sweet and friendly. It wasn't long after we had started our friendship that they were evicted. They would no longer be close and I knew that this would affect my community-building efforts. And it did. Unfortunately, that is part of the game. Not everyone you meet will be able to be in your corner. Sometimes it's their choosing, your choosing, or it just doesn't work out. Don't take it personally, just keep moving forward.

The second "C" is Calling. This is also known as your purpose. There's an acronym that I like to use from Rick Warren to help me navigate this - S.H.A.P.E. "S" stands for spiritual gifts. "H" stands for heart. "A" is for abilities. "P" is your personality.

"E" is for life experiences. Now, this isn't necessarily a test that you take and it spits out what you are supposed to do with your lift. Rather, it gives you a sense of what your positive strengths are, things you should avoid, and guide you to types of things that you would probably do well in or not worry about.

I have seen this concept work over and over again with individuals because of my time as a pastor, but I had never put myself on the other side of the table. The honest to God truth was, I didn't know my purpose or my calling. I didn't think it was what it used to be. My life has shifted. However, that doesn't mean that I don't have one because I know I do. I'm currently in a "searching mode". I'm reevaluating where I am now, how I have changed, and where I fit in this world now. Maybe this book has something to do with it. I don't know, but I'm going to continue to work on this part of my journey. My life has been spent navigating wildfires. However, who knows what can vibrantly grow out of the ashes?

Conversations. We have them every single day. Small talk with the coffee barista, cashiers, waitress or waiters, or maybe even your cat. But this isn't actually a *conversation*. When I say "conversation" I mean deep emotional and vulnerable topics, open hearts, active listening, and extended time mulling the topic over together. It's connection. It's getting down to the depths of the soul. It's going to probably make you anxious. Your palms will probably sweat. You might be filled with panic. But with those conversations comes healing, growth, and community. We all need to share our stories - the good, the bad, and the ugly. Choose your uncomfortable. You can be uncomfortable in your loneliness or you can be uncomfortable opening up to someone with the hopes of finding fertilizer for your ashes.

When I was at Bristol, the hospice company I worked for in Hawaii, a major part of my job was to sit and listen to my patients that were preparing to leave this world and help them navigate any lingering issues - anger, resentment, etc. - and find closure and peace. One day while in this role, I approached a beautiful town house. I knocked on the door and a man opened the door. I explained what I was doing there and he gestured to the back bedroom. I took my shoes off and walked into the dim bedroom, only lit with one lamp next to the bed. Mary was sitting there in the bed looking at me. I couldn't help but think this was the most awkward situation in the world. Here I am, a random shoeless man standing at her bedside. So, I decided I would just break the icy tension with that. I said, "Mary, I bet this is awkward." She smiled slightly and completely agreed. I continued, "Let me tell you about why I'm here."

She responded, "I know. I know."

In a genuine tone I asked, "What do you know?"

She looked at me filled with a ball of different emotions. "I'm gonna... I talked to the doctors this morning and he said " I'm gonna..." She couldn't get out the word "die".

"What are you going to do, Mary?" She refused to think that she was going to die. Although it has been medically confirmed, she believed that somehow she would be miraculously healed. She was fighting and fighting against the entire concept. Eventually in the conversation, I got her to say the word. It was a huge moment of realization.

"Am I going to die?" she weakly questioned.

I had to answer her, "Yes, you are going to die, but let's make the best of the rest of your life." Through this continuing deep level conversation that she expressed she had a lot of resentment and anger toward her husband. Throughout the marriage, she would go out drinking at night. When she would come home, he would then go out when she really just wanted him to stay home with her. This repetitive situation caused many arguments and a lasting anger that continued to build. This on top of financial and communication issues, had resulted in a marriage fueled with bitterness. I suggested that we should work together through the anger and the money concerns.

"What do you mean?" she asked.

"Forgiveness," I answered.

"No way!" she insisted.

I said, "I'm not asking you to forgive him. I'm just asking you to think about it. To just consider what it would do. Forgiveness isn't really about him. Forgiveness is about you letting go of the offense that he did to you. Holding on to all of that is going to make you more angry, right?"

"I never...I never...I never thought of it that way before," she pondered.

We continued this deep conversation that day and over the next several visits. I was able to just be fully present and help her navigate those feelings. Before she passed away, she was actually able to talk with her husband, forgive him, apologize for her wrong doings, and find peace before she lost her ability to speak. This story displays the pure power of taking the time to dig into those hard things in our life. Not just burying things, waiting on a clock, distracting yourself, until it just "goes away". You can't go around it until you go through it.

Finally, this brings us to Cultivation. This is where we see all the other pieces come together. This part starts as being a lifelong learner by taking in anything you can get your hands on, books, articles, podcasts, shows, etc. By understanding new things and combining them with your previous lessons and life experiences, you will grow. The beneficial thing about seeking out new things is that you will naturally find people that are learning the same thing - which could be an outlet to connect you to your community. Now, you're not just working on yourself by yourself, but rather working on yourself with someone else. We're walking this path together, having quality conversations, supporting each other. When you stumble, they are there to help you. When they stumble, you're there to help them. Then together, you both figure out what your purpose is. All these pieces together put you on a path to a healthier life.

I've been learning a lot about depression and suicidal ideation by reading, watching videos, and attending seminars. I recently attended a seminar called the American Foundation for Suicidal Prevention. Every Saturday after Thanksgiving, they have a "Survivors of Loss Day". This is a day when people who have lost someone in their life to suicide can come together and find a community with a shared similar experience. I had first heard about this foundation back in Hawaii when I saw someone with a t-shirt that said "#stopsuicide". I immediately went over to him and found out he was the voluntary leader of the local chapter of the associate. I went back to his table with him where there were a few other board members who were planning that event. We were visiting and he offered to pick me up, take me to the event, and take me back home. Turns out, it was and has continued to be a powerful experience. I go, even though I haven't lost someone, but rather because I was going to be the one lost. Throughout the seminar, people would ask me who I lost. As I explained each time that it was actually me, you wouldn't have believed the love, connection, and instant support that is given by each and every person every single time. It isn't a mushy gushy scene, but rather the right amount of "We hear you. We see you. We love you. We've got you."

These four topics aren't necessarily a list or steps in a certain order that will solve all your problems tomorrow. Rather, this is a spiraling system that continuously builds upon itself to set you up for a healthier lift. Will it work for everyone? I have no idea. But I do know, I have seen it work for others and it is currently working for me. At the end of the day, we have to do something. Sweeping our hurt, our anger, our traumas, our lives under the rug isn't doing us any favors. It's time to start taking care of those dirt piles that are making our rugs so lumpy.

You might think by now that I would have lost my faith in God. Depression has affected every facet of my life. It has shattered my hopes and dreams, time and time again. Sometimes I think, *Everything feels so useless. Why go on? Why don't I just throw in the towel and quit?* But I haven't thrown in the towel. I haven't quit. And I know, I have not lost my faith in God.

Every day is a constant struggle, a battle, to exercise that faith. This book bears witness to my struggle and my faith, and through it, I extend my hand to whomever may read it. Maybe, as you read this, I have helped you understand that you are not alone in your own struggle, or that someone you know may be silently struggling with an invisible illness and needs your love and support. As I look forward, I am hopeful for the next chapter of my life to begin. As I work through each day, I keep the words of my friend Dave close at hand, and I send them to you: *Remember... Don't do it today, you can do it tomorrow.*

I often think of Bill Wilson, founder of Alcoholics Anonymous. He went in and out of treatment but would always relapse until one day he greeted someone with the iconic saying, "Hello, I'm Bill and I'm an alcoholic." That moment caused him to be strong enough to not need to drink again.

Anytime he would meet someone and say that introduction, he noticed he didn't need a drink that day and he got stronger.

I personally don't feel the need to go around shaking people's hands and saying, "Hello, I'm John and I'm a depressed man with suicidal ideation." However, I can write a book that says that and more. I can make the invisible visible by telling my story. My memoir has the potential to reach people who are struggling with the same illness, who also feel invisible and misunderstood, and who need to hear that they are not alone. It could also reach people who do not struggle with depression, but who most certainly know someone who is: a coworker, a friend, a family member, a student. My story could remind them that not all illnesses can be seen, that we can never assume to know what someone is enduring inside, that very real pain and affliction can, and does, hide in plain sight every day.

I may not know where my life is going. But I do know one thing. And this one thing is the only thing that is truly keeping me alive. Despite everything, I know there is still love in me that needs to be given away. I say that purposely because it reminds me of the quote from Oscar Hammerstein:

A bell's not a bell 'til you ring it.
A song's not a song 'til you sing it.
Love in your heart wasn't put there to stay.
Love isn't love 'til you give it away.

I don't know what that love inside me is for, but I do know that it's meant to be given away. To who? To you, reader, for a start. Beyond that, I don't know yet. All I know is that I can't kill love.

About the Author

John Miller, DMin has had a varied career in ministry.

He secured his BA Pastoral Ministry from Southeastern University and has MAs in Christian Ministry and Clinical Counseling from the Assemblies of God Theological Seminary and Regent University, respectively. John received his doctorate from Assemblies of God Theological Seminary.

John has served as a Staff Pastor, a Hospice Chaplain, a conference Speaker at international gatherings, and has raised over $150,000 in mission's projects.

Outside of ministry, John is a 49ers fan for life and enjoys watching Brazilian Jiu Jitsu. He has two boys, Jaxson and Jentzen.

Ingram Content Group UK Ltd.
Milton Keynes UK
UKHW020201040523
421194UK00019B/189/J

9 798822 914407